I0483401

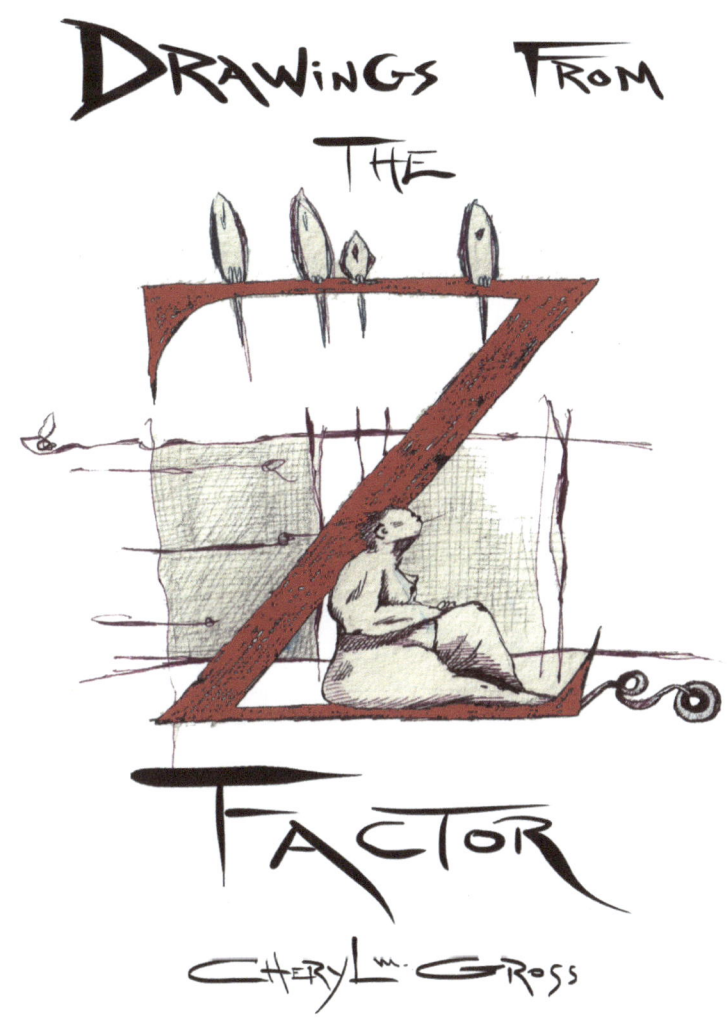

DRAWINGS FROM THE Z FACTOR

Cheryl M. Gross

VICTORY HALL PRESS

April 2014
Victory Hall Press
ISBN-13: 978-0615993713
ISBN-10: 0615993710
Copyright 2014
Editor: James Pustorino
website: www.victoryhallpress.org

contact: victoryhall1@msn.com

Victory Hall Inc. 74 W 46 St
Bayonne, NJ 07002
www.victoryhall.org

This program is made possible in part by funds from the New Jersey State Council on the Arts/Department of State, a partner agency of the National Endowment for the Arts, administered by the Hudson County Office of Cultural and Heritage Affairs, Thomas A. Degise, County Executive, and the Board of Chosen Freeholders.

Drawings from The Z Factor

The Z Factor is a compelling story of how three generations
involved in the creation of a new species of premeditated
human evolution, consequently altered the future of the world,
as we know it…forever.

Beginning at the later part of the 19th Century, *The Z Factor*
takes us on an historical journey throughout some of the most
monumental movements in modern art. It carries the reader into
our postmodern subsistence, and paves the way to an
exceedingly surprising and unsettling future.

Drawings from The Z Factor is a compilation of the original
color illustrations and quotes from the novel.

Follow your dreams, except that one where you're naked in church.

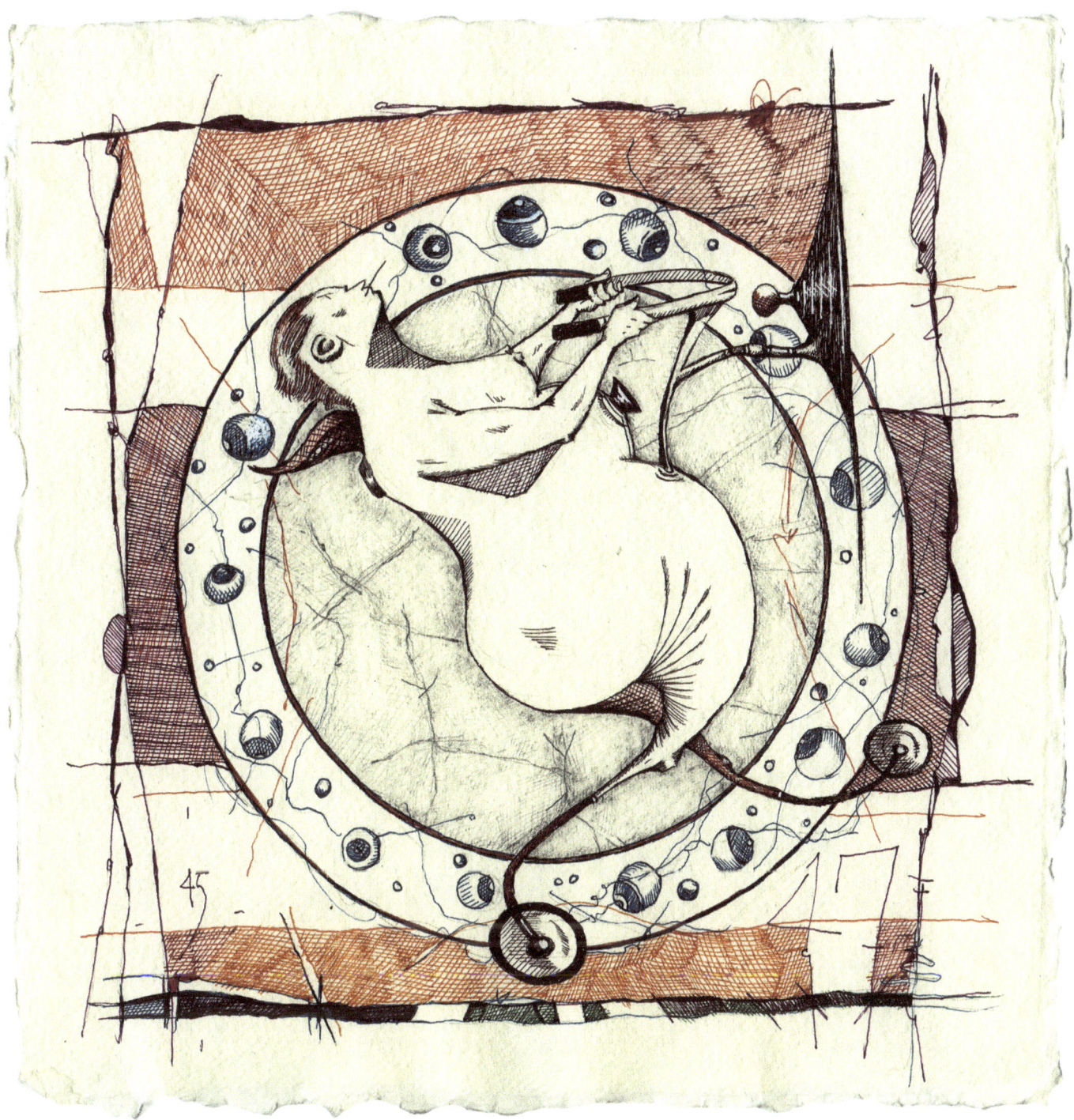

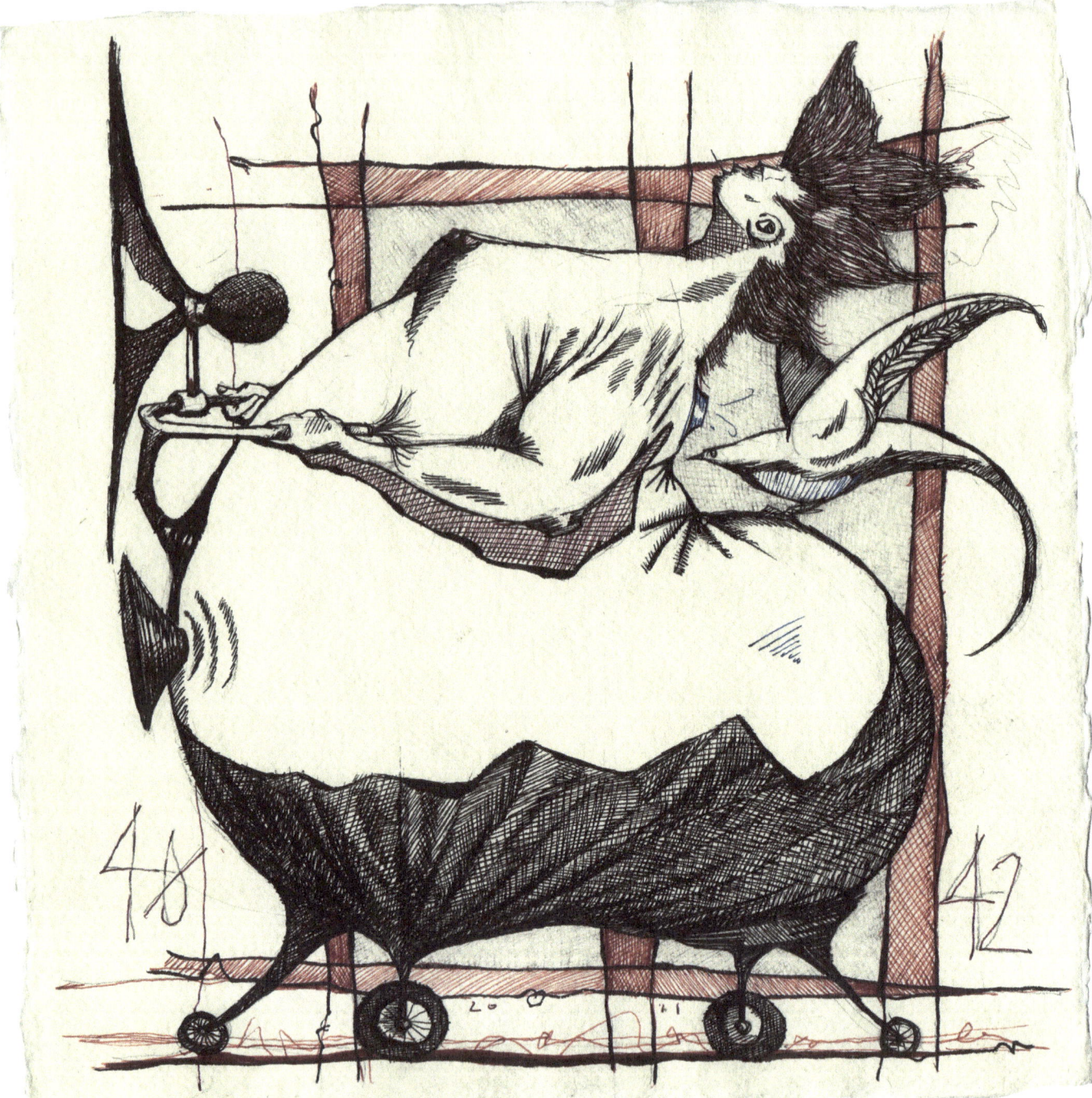

I'm not your type. I'm not inflatable.

Kinky is using a feather. Perverted is using the whole chicken.

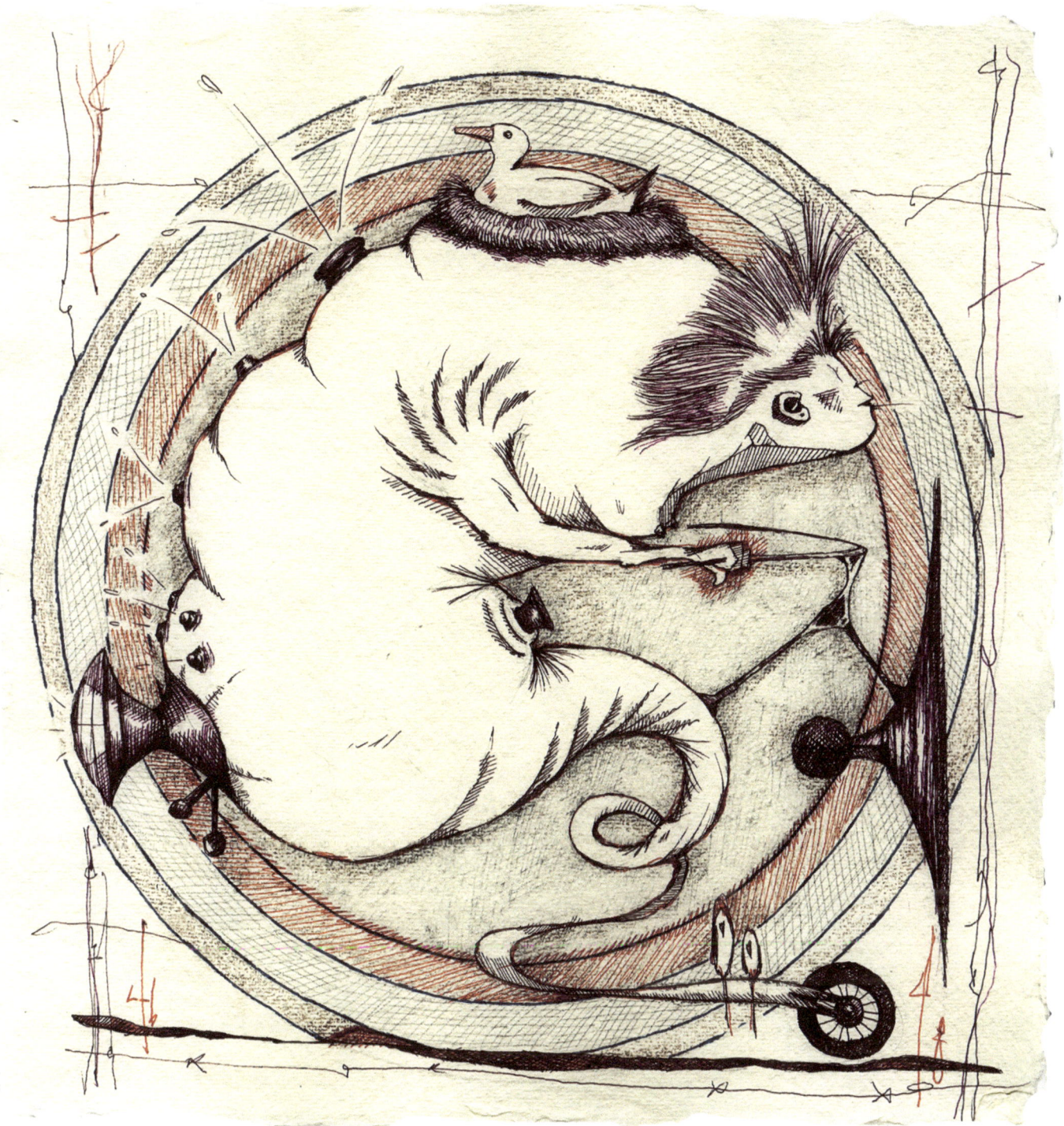

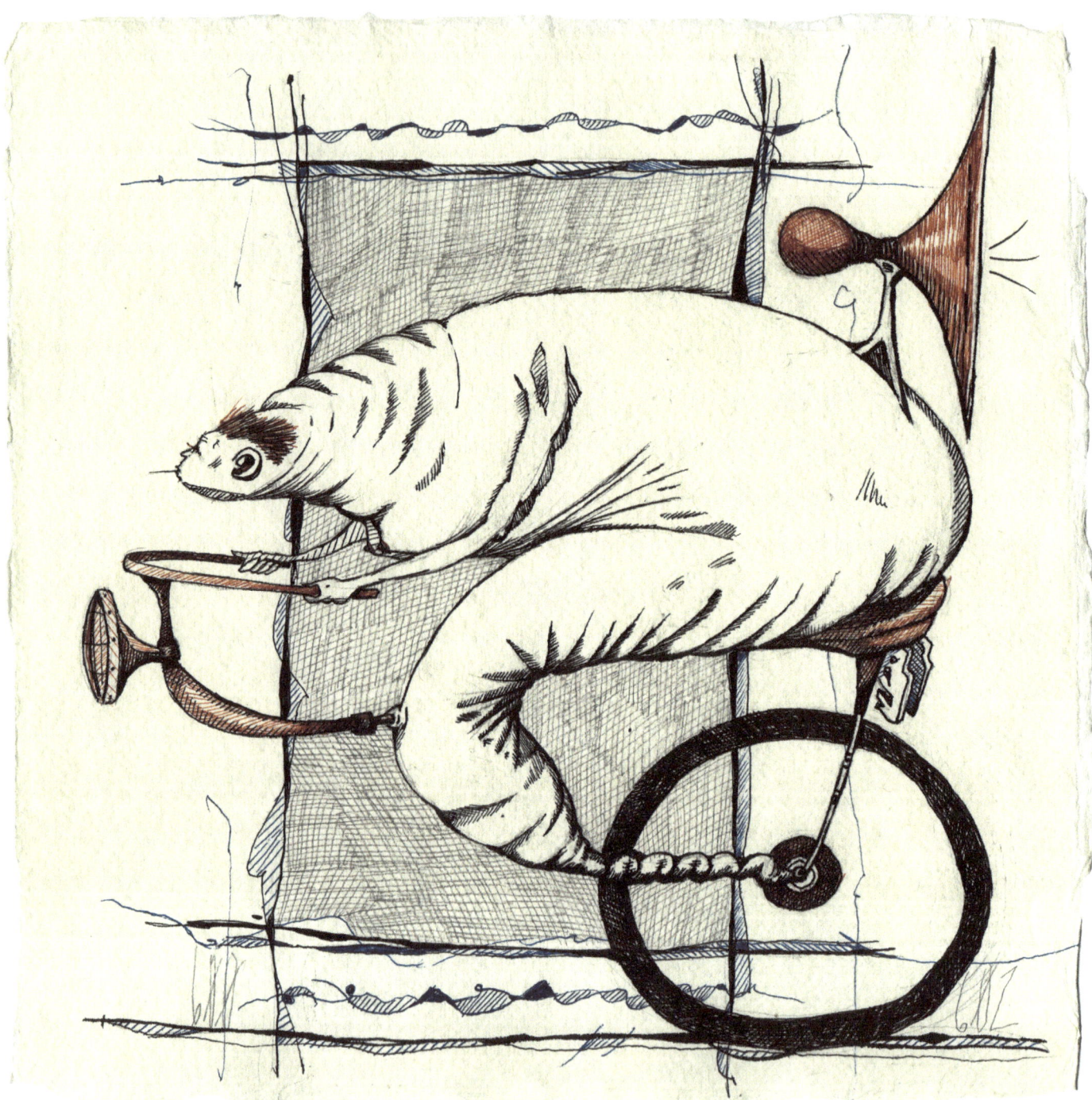

Never hold your farts in. They travel up your spine into your brain
and that's where shitty ideas come from.

Don't take candy from strangers unless they offer you a ride.

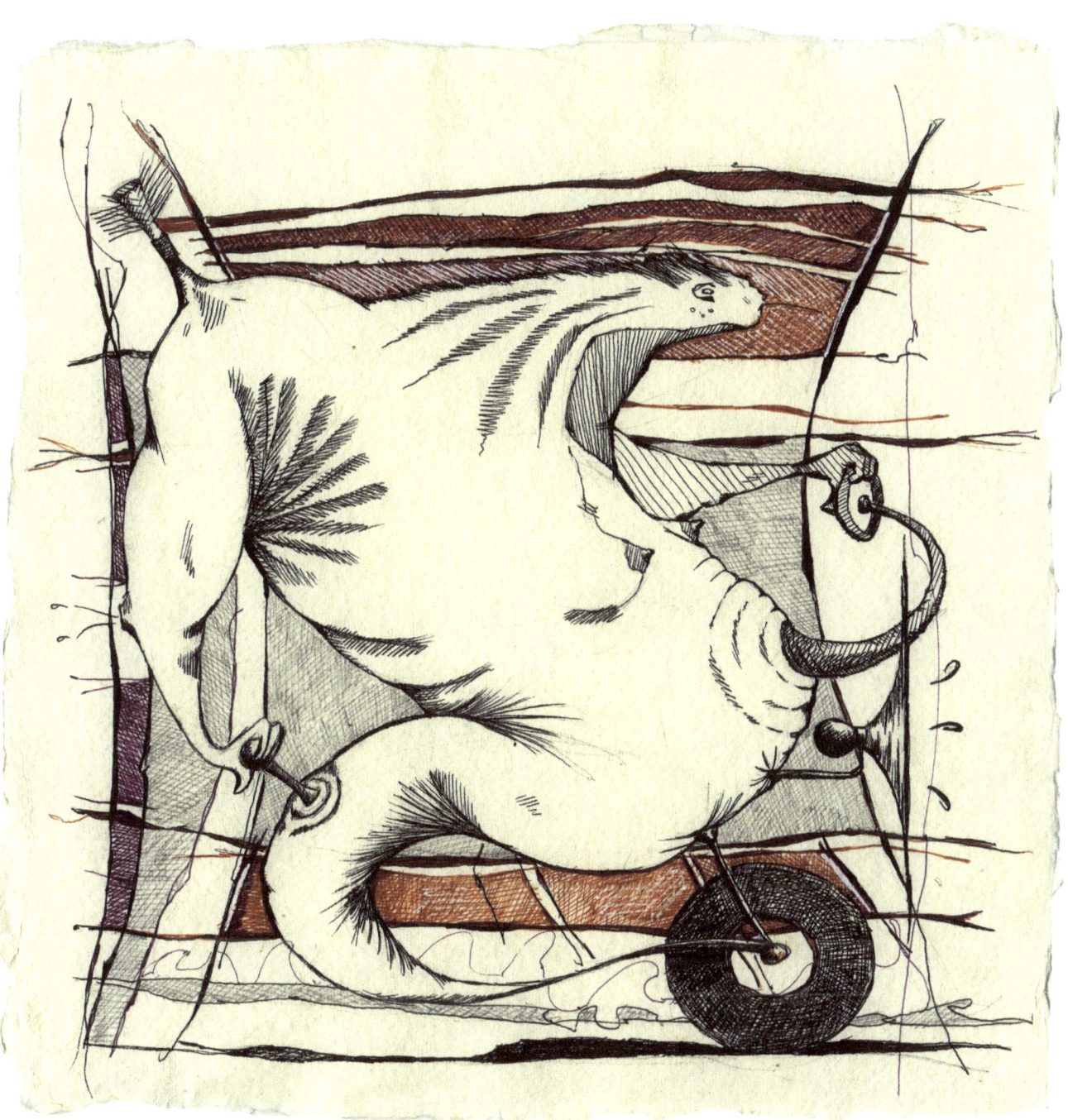

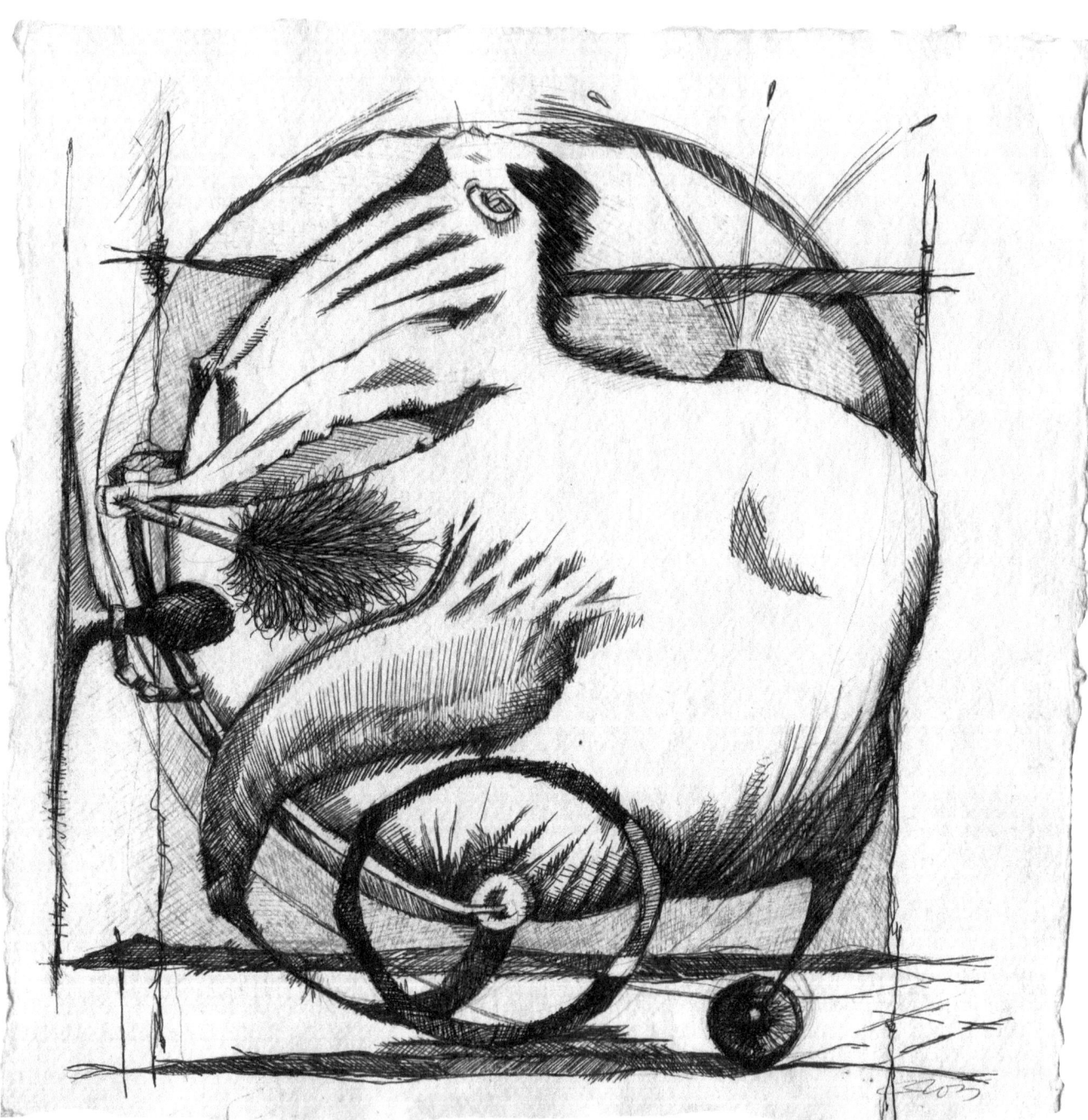

He who thinks by the inch and talks by the yard should
be kicked in the foot.

Children are our future, unless we stop them now!

Homer Simpson

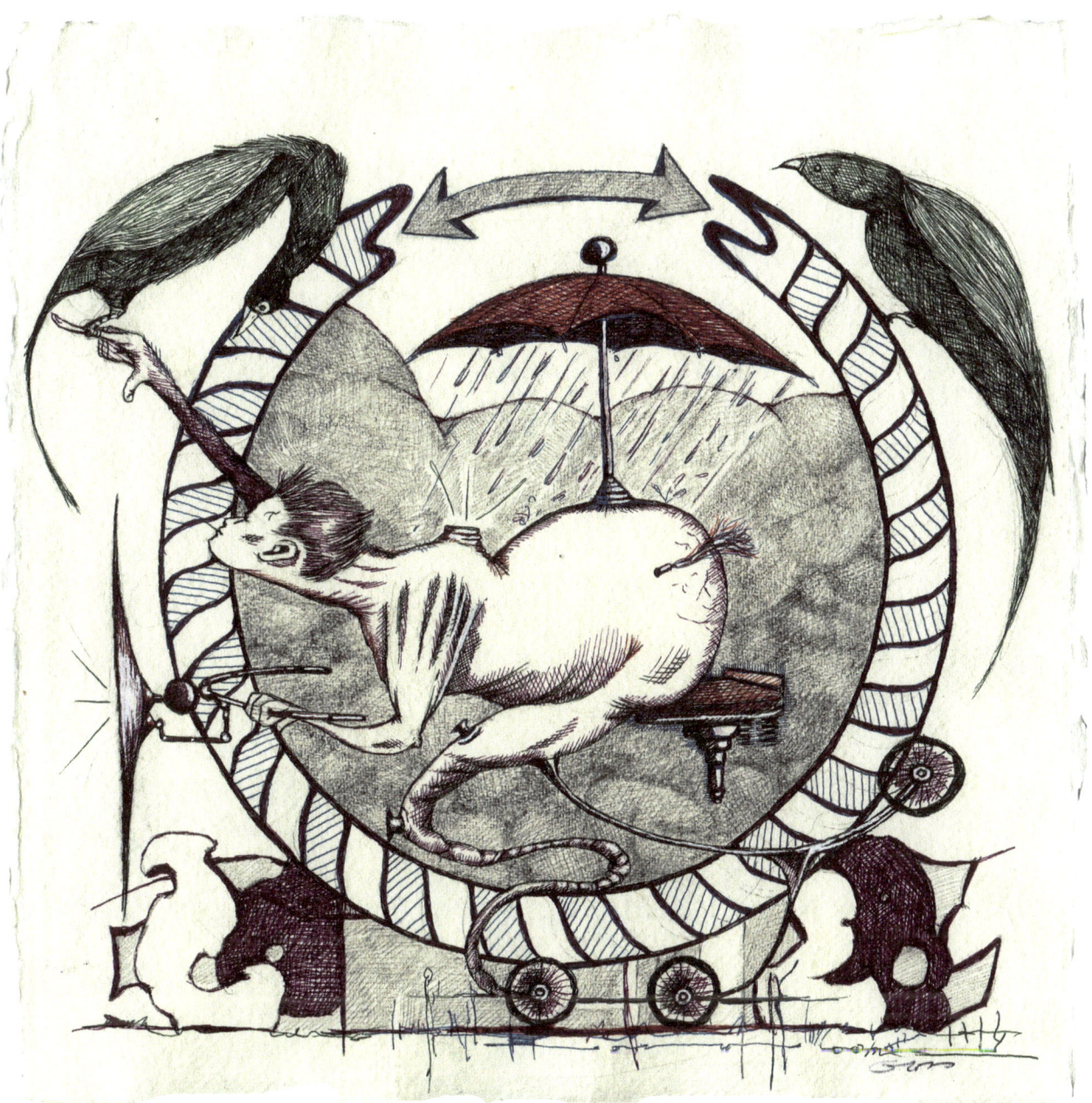

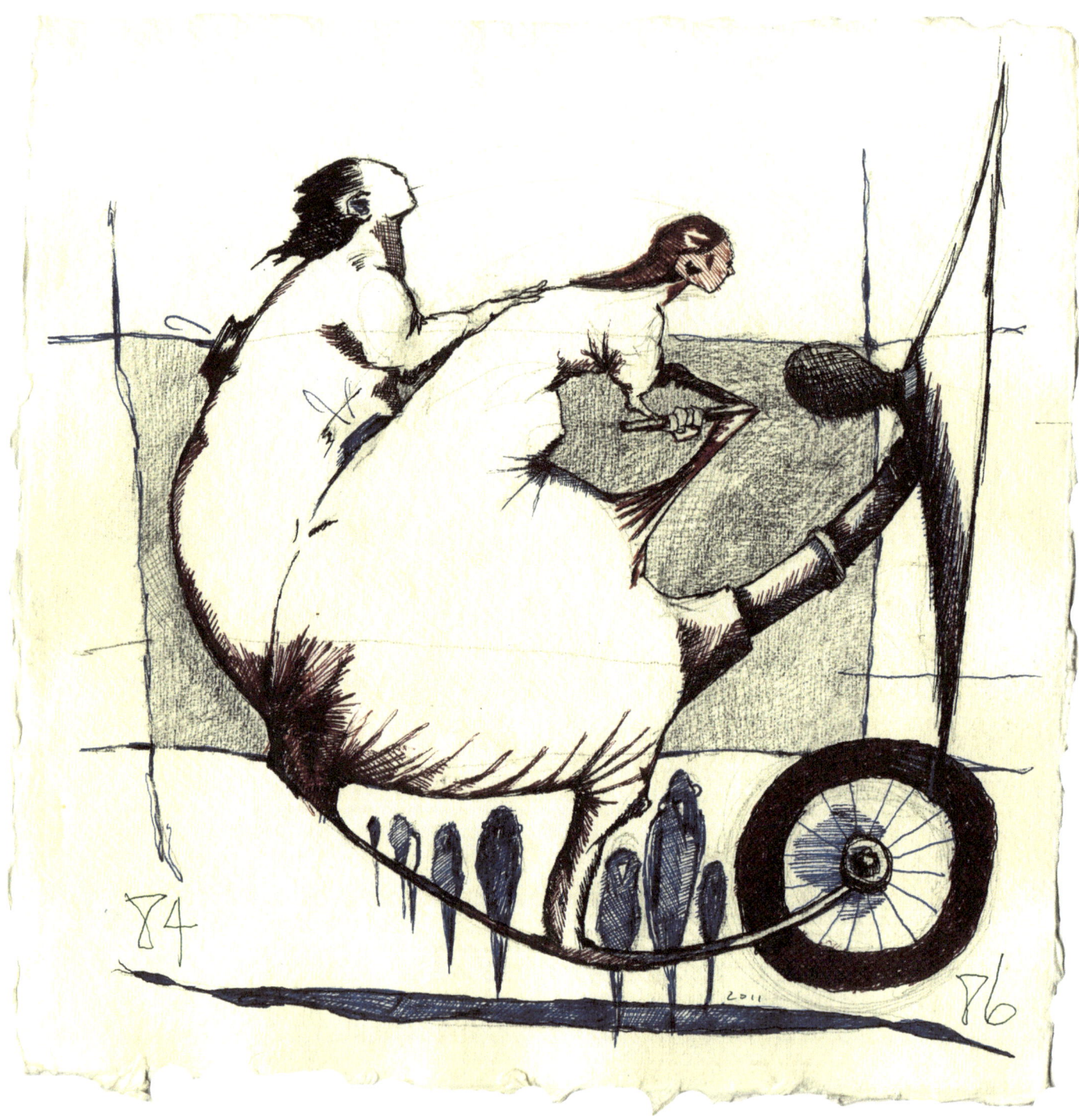

84

2011

86

Any connection to your reality and mine is purely coincidental.

Out of my mind, be back in five minutes.

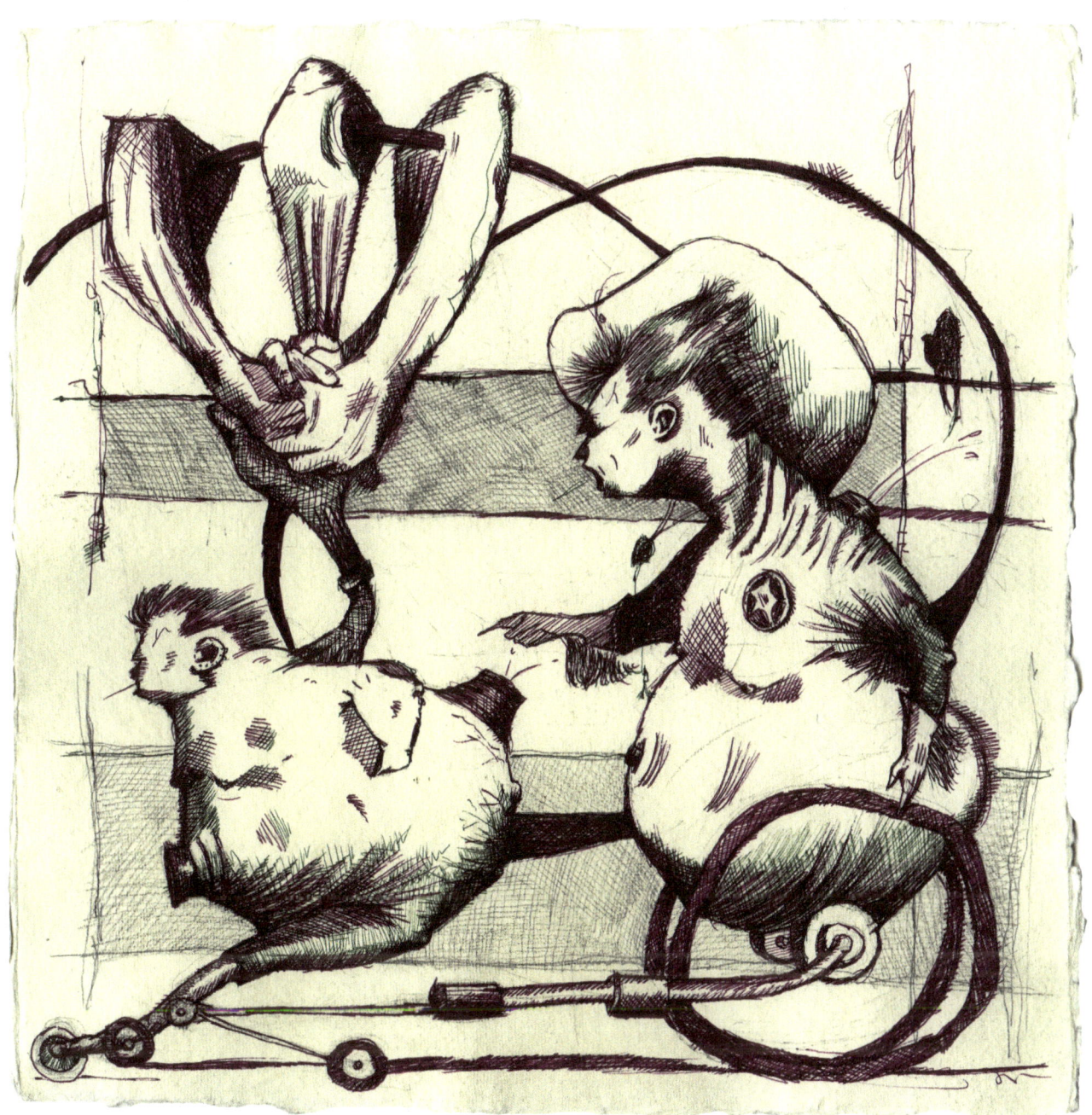

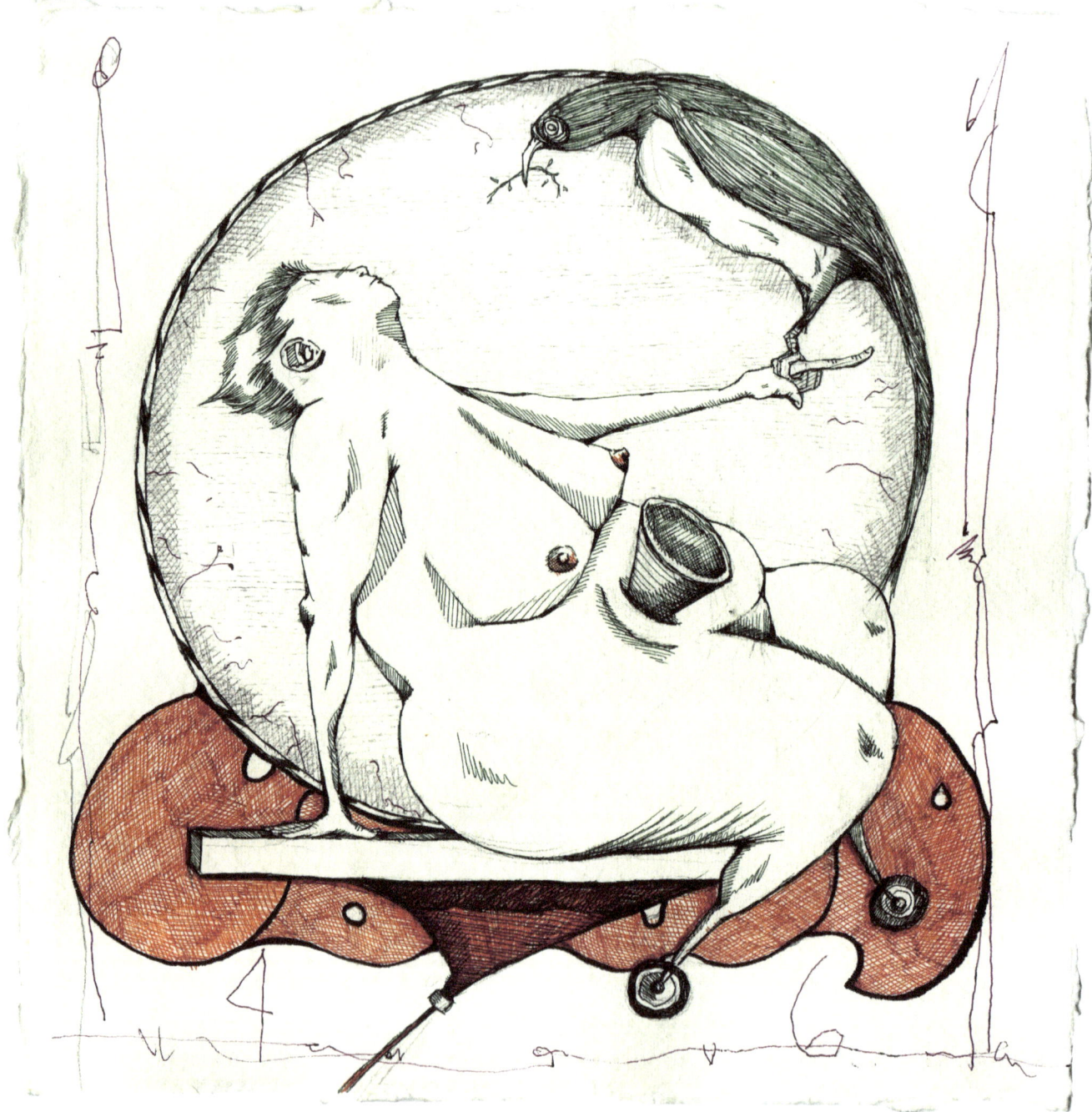

I found Jesus! He was in the trunk of my car when I got back from Tijuana.

We now return to your life, already in progress.

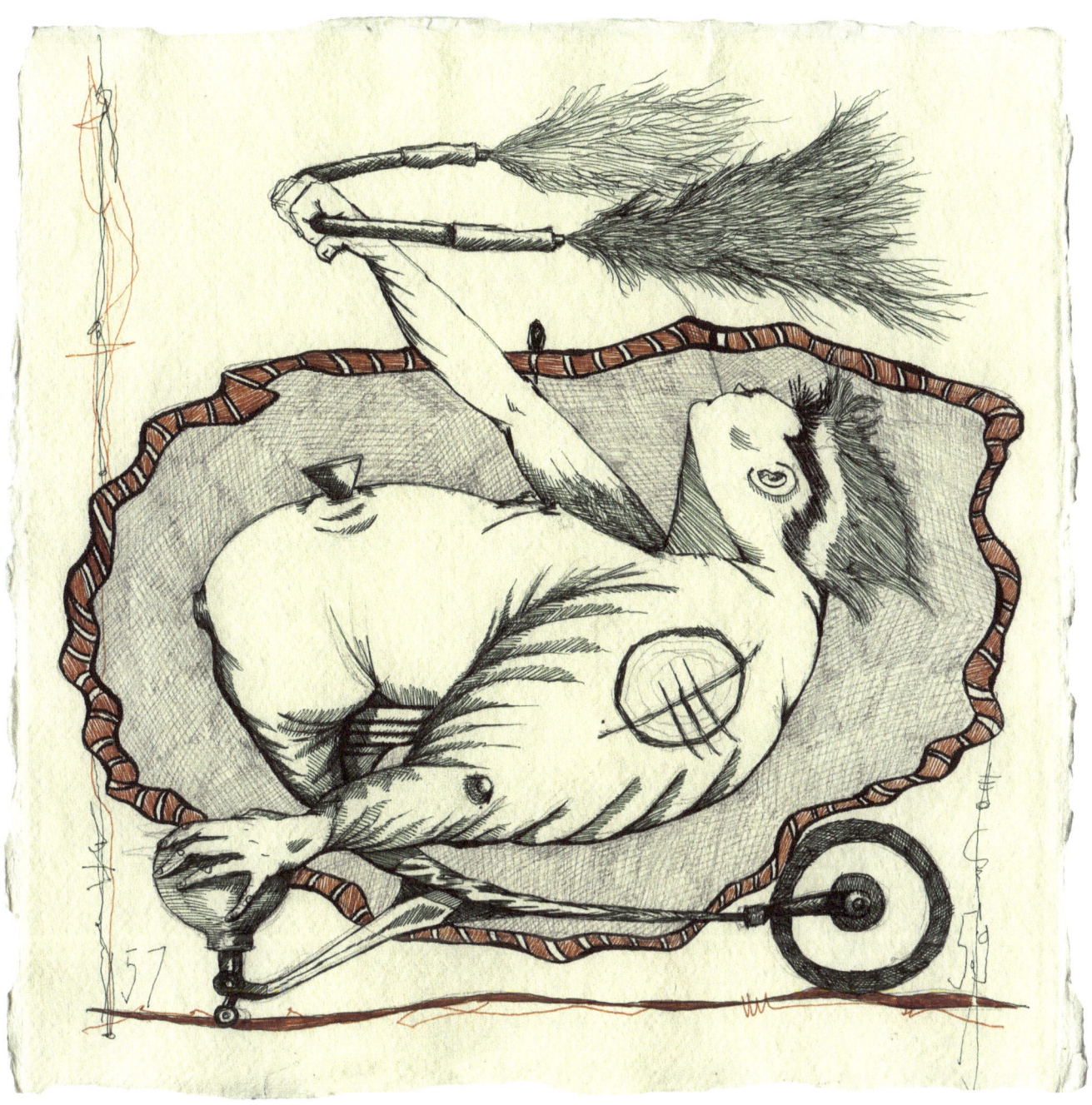

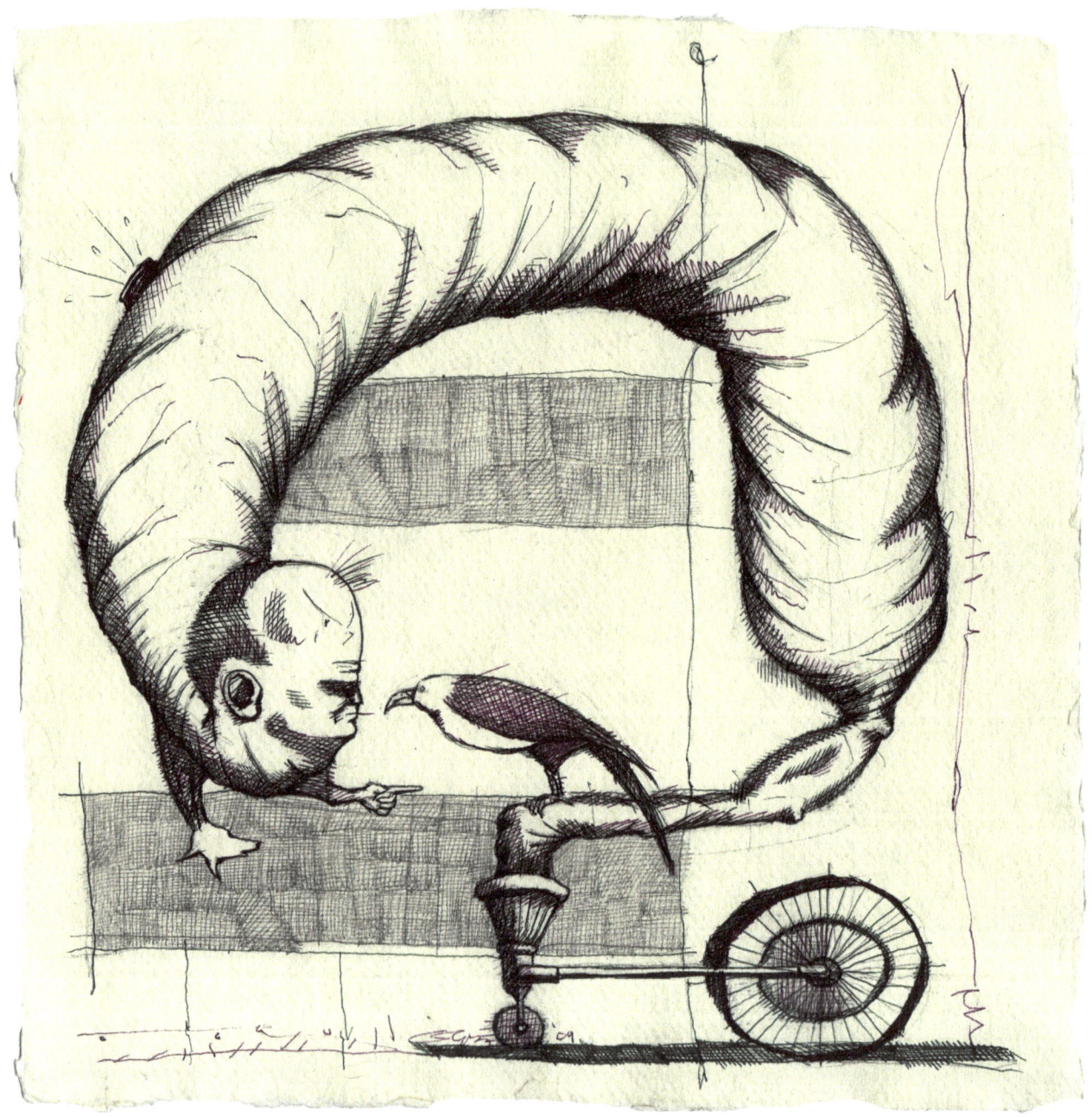

Yesterday is just a memory, tomorrow is only a dream,
but today is a real bitch.

Artificial intelligence is no match for real stupidity.

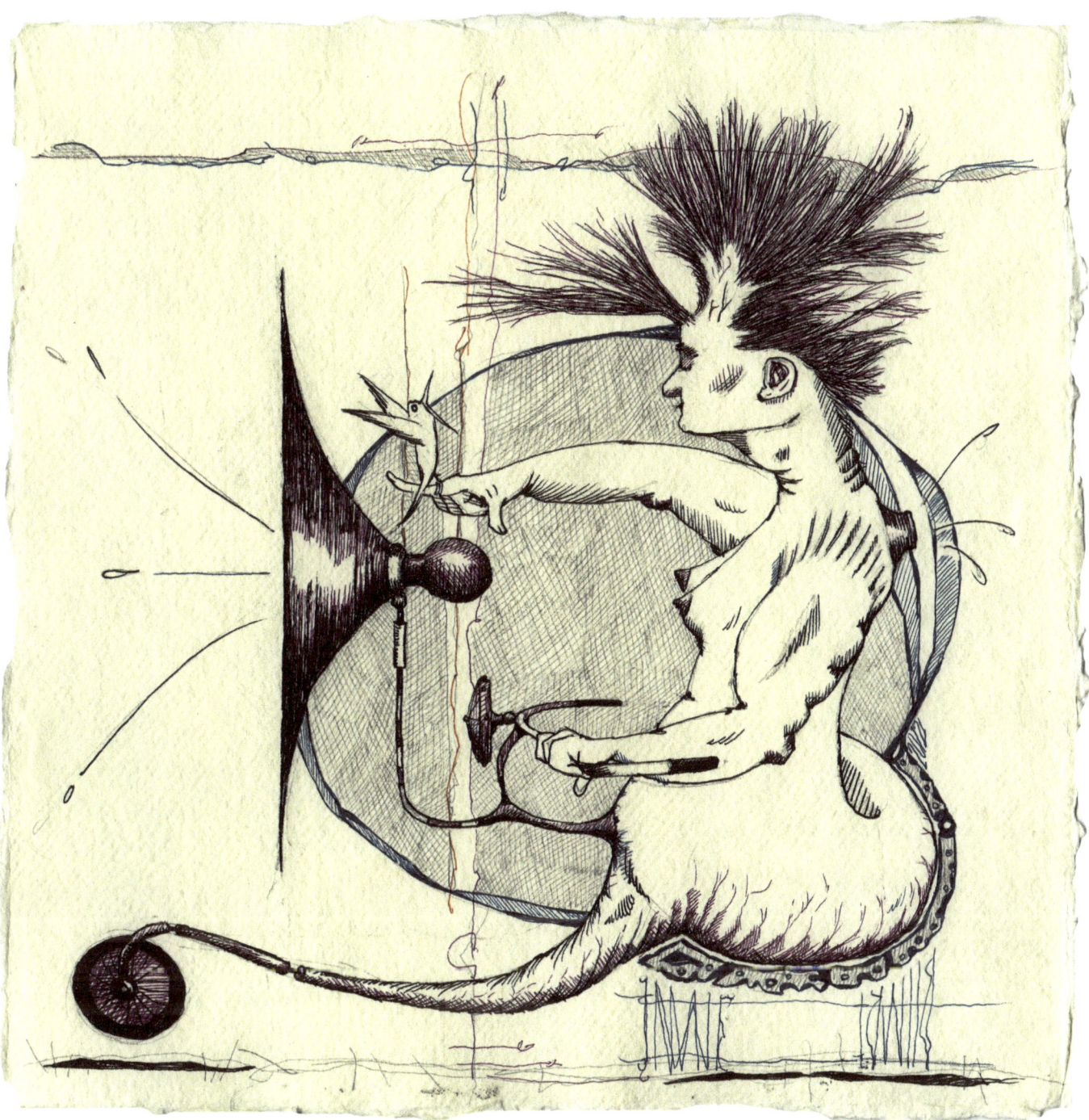

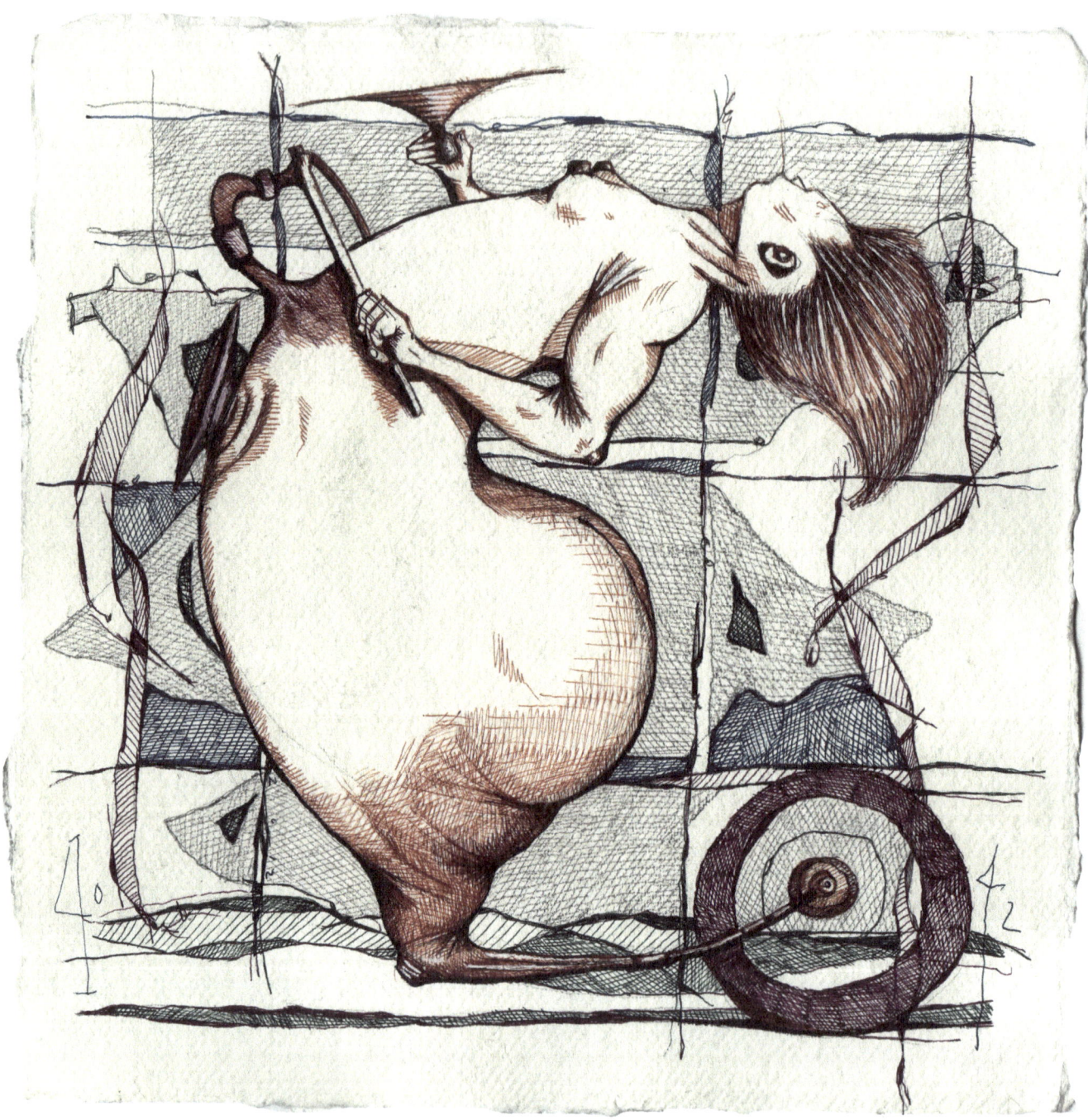

Everyone has a photographic memory; some just don't have film.

Steven Wright

Don't rub the lamp unless you're ready for the genie.

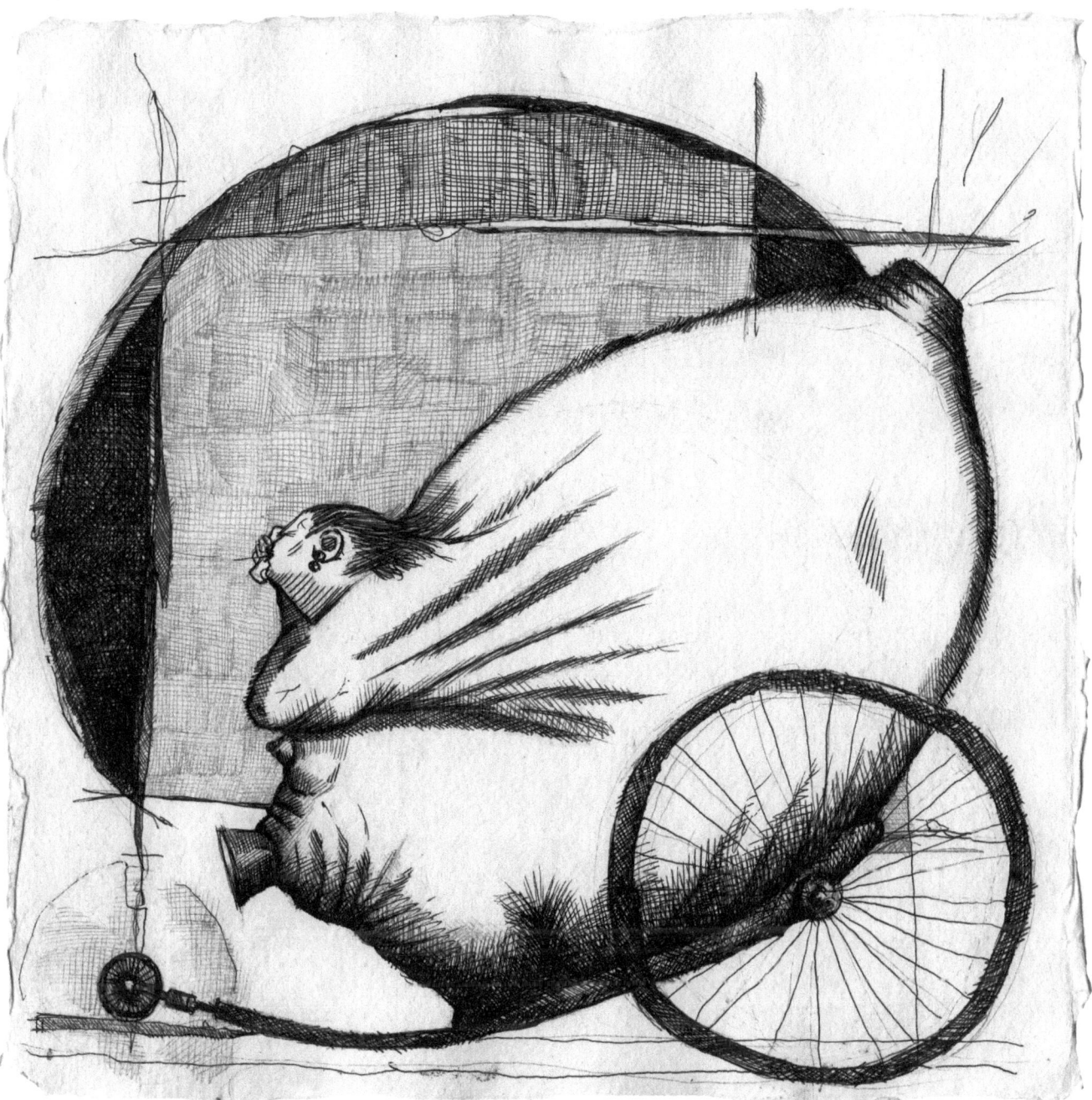

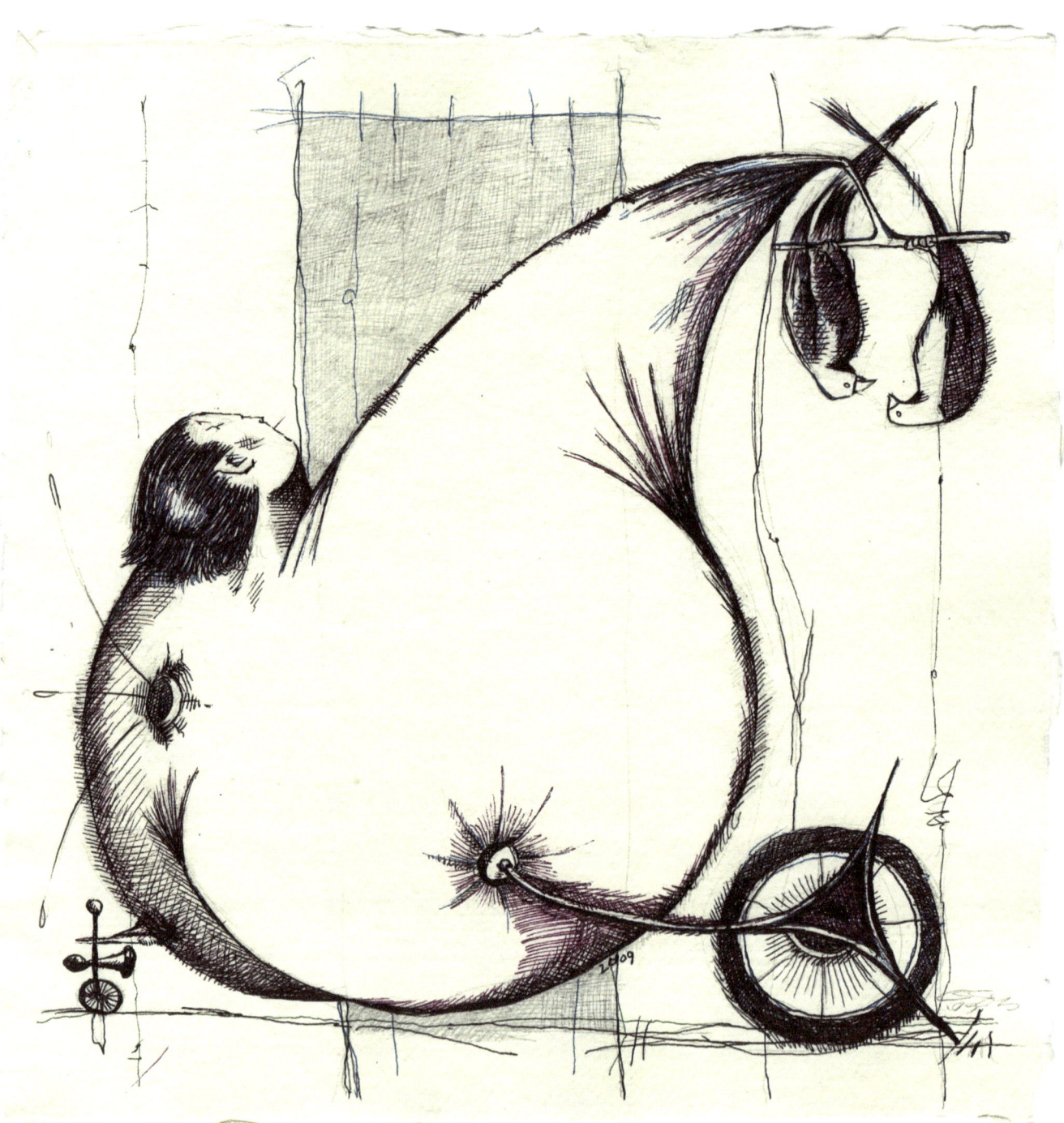

A closed mouth gathers no feet.

The road to success is always under construction.

Lily Tomlin

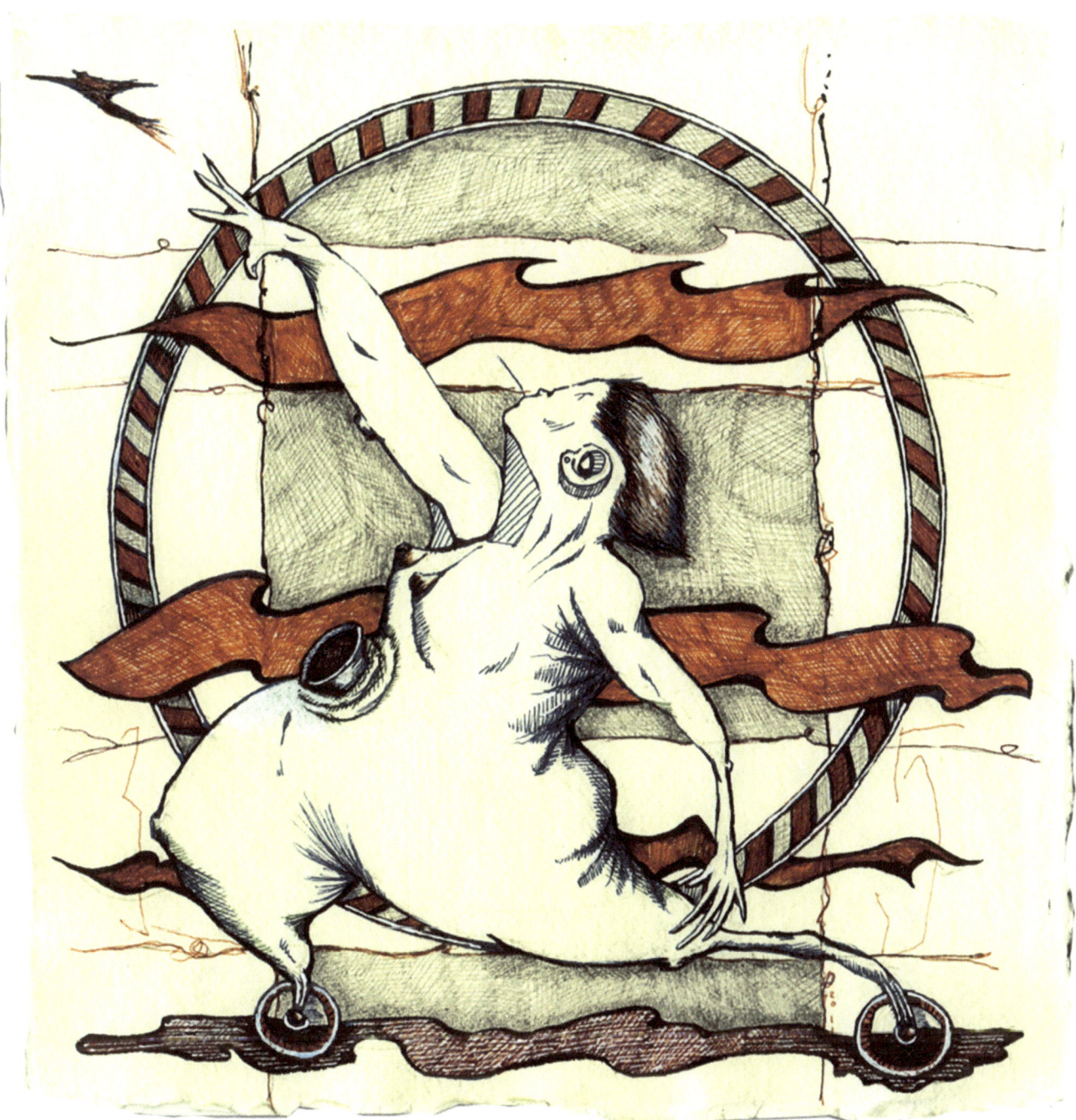

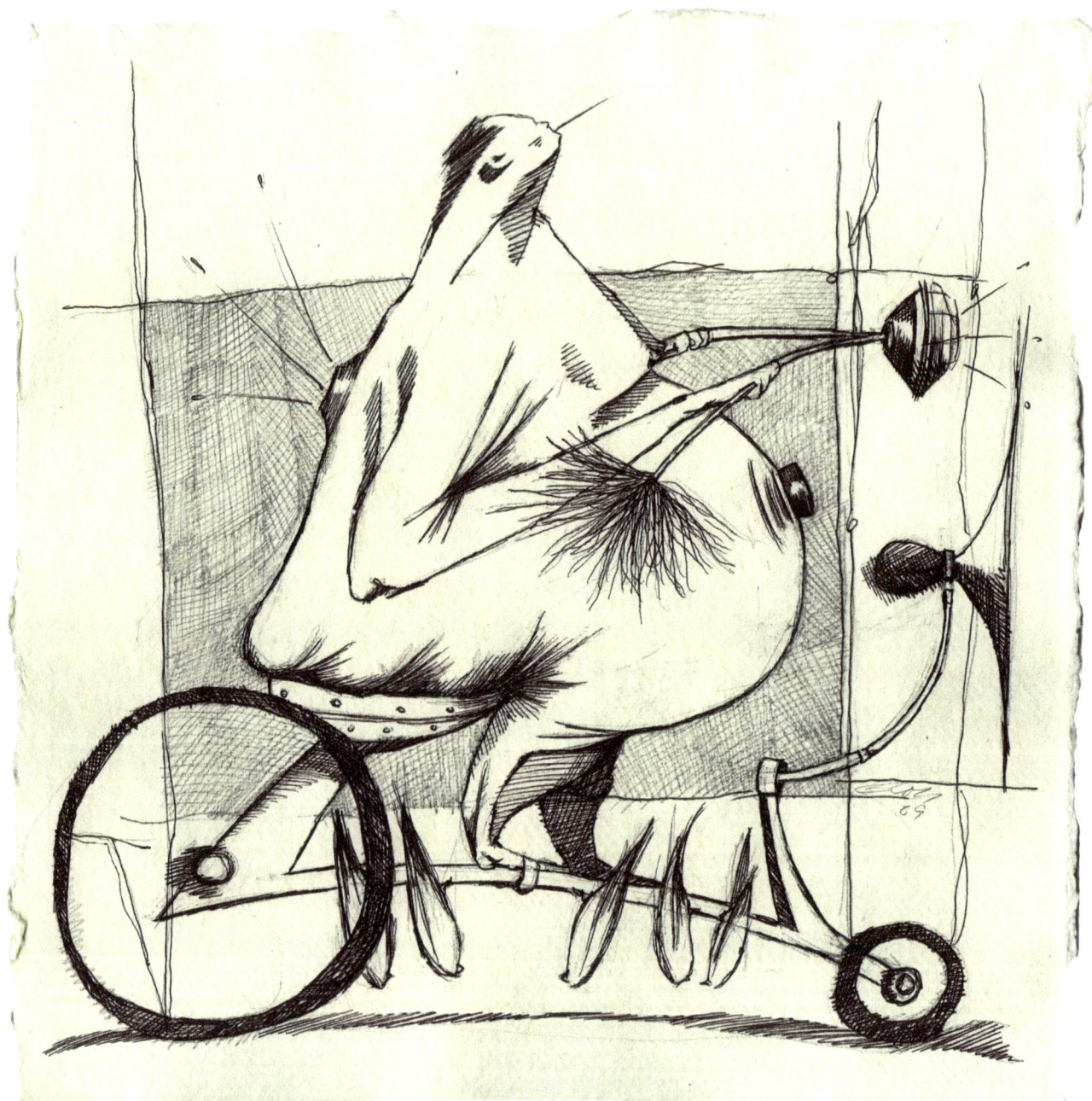

*Inside every older person is a younger person wondering
what the hell happened.*

Cora Harvey Armstrong

When you go to trial, you're putting yourself in the hands
of twelve people that weren't smart enough to get out of jury duty.

Norm Crosby

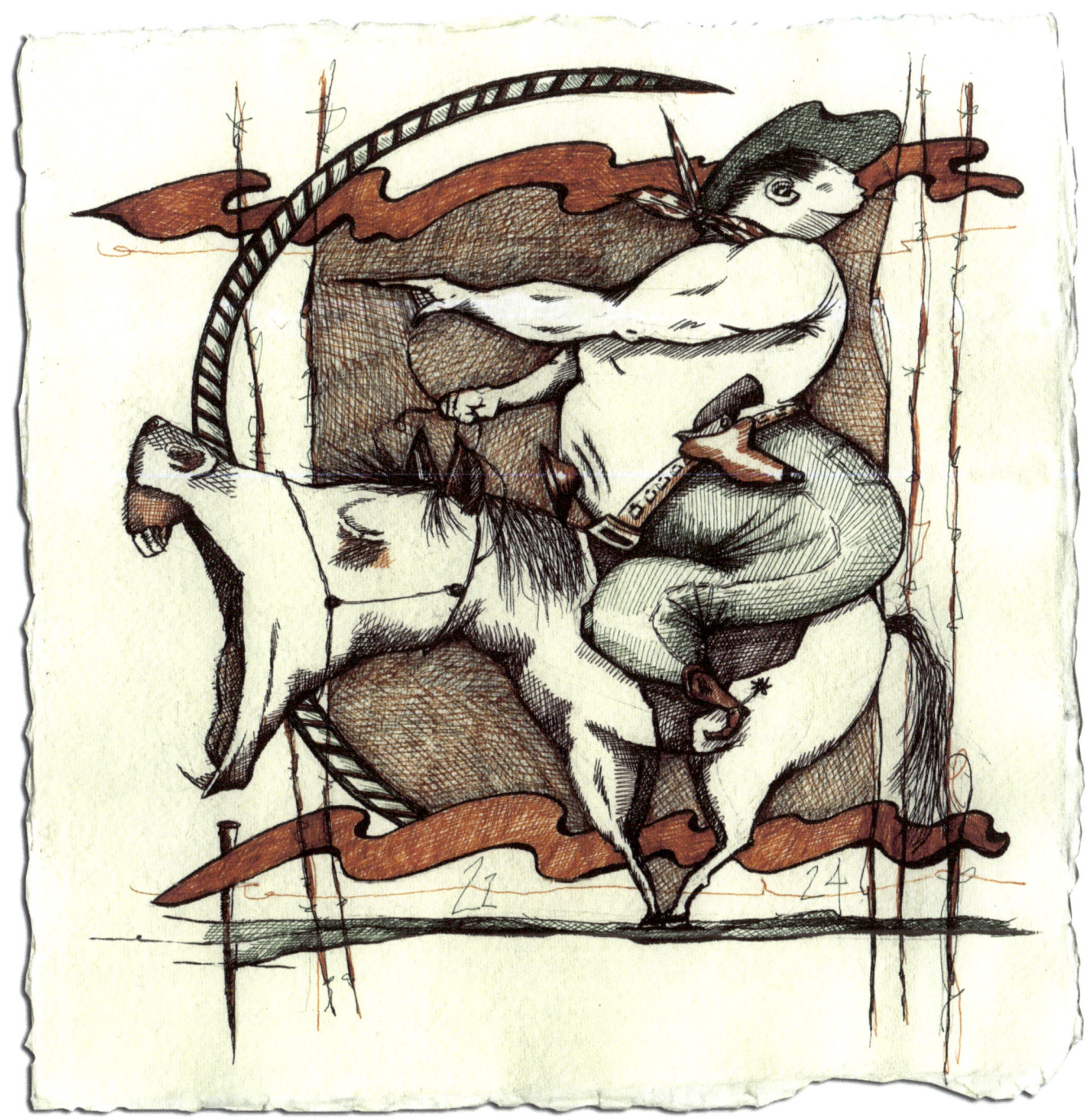

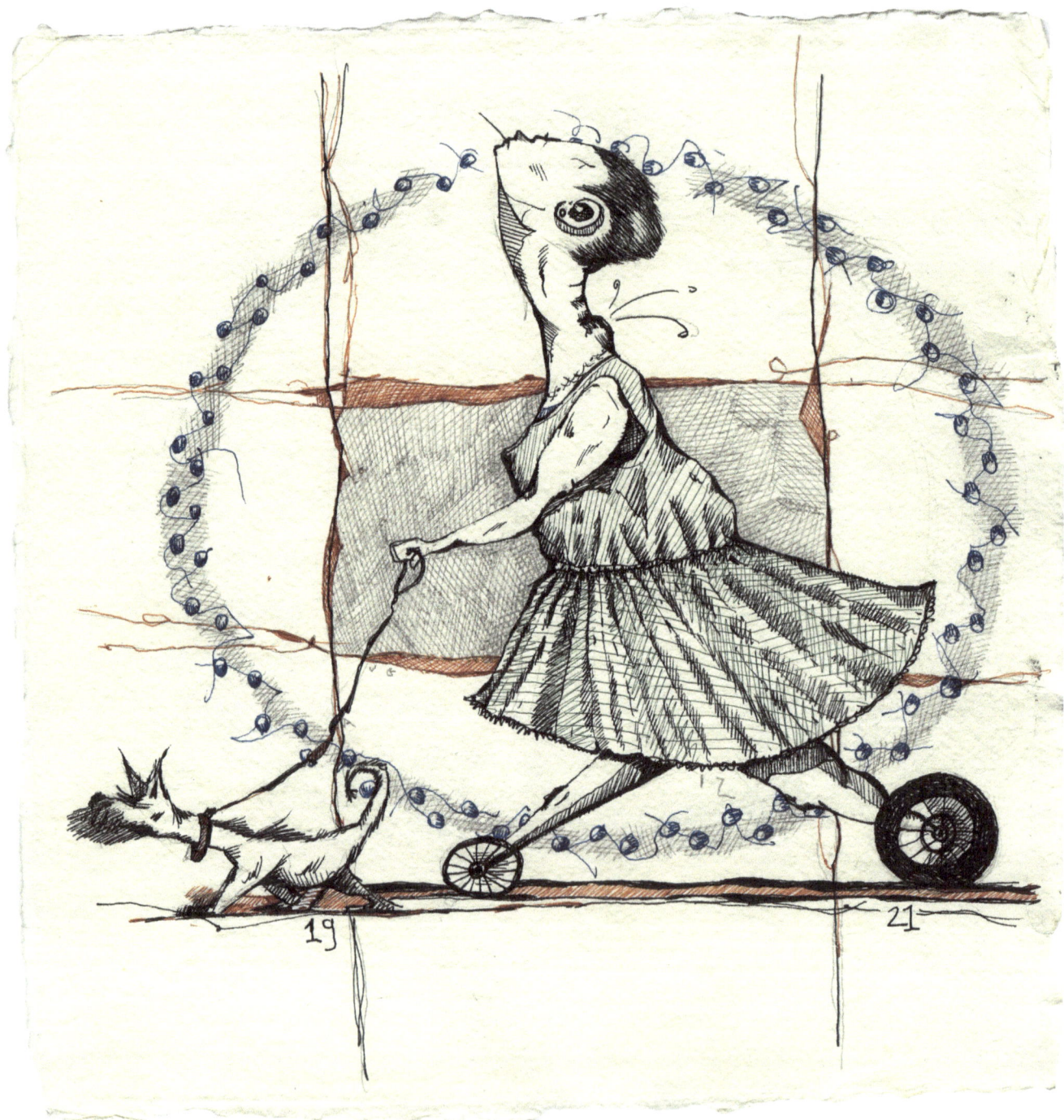

I used to have an open mind but my brains kept falling out.

Steven Wright

Silence is golden, but duck tape is silver.

Against All Authority

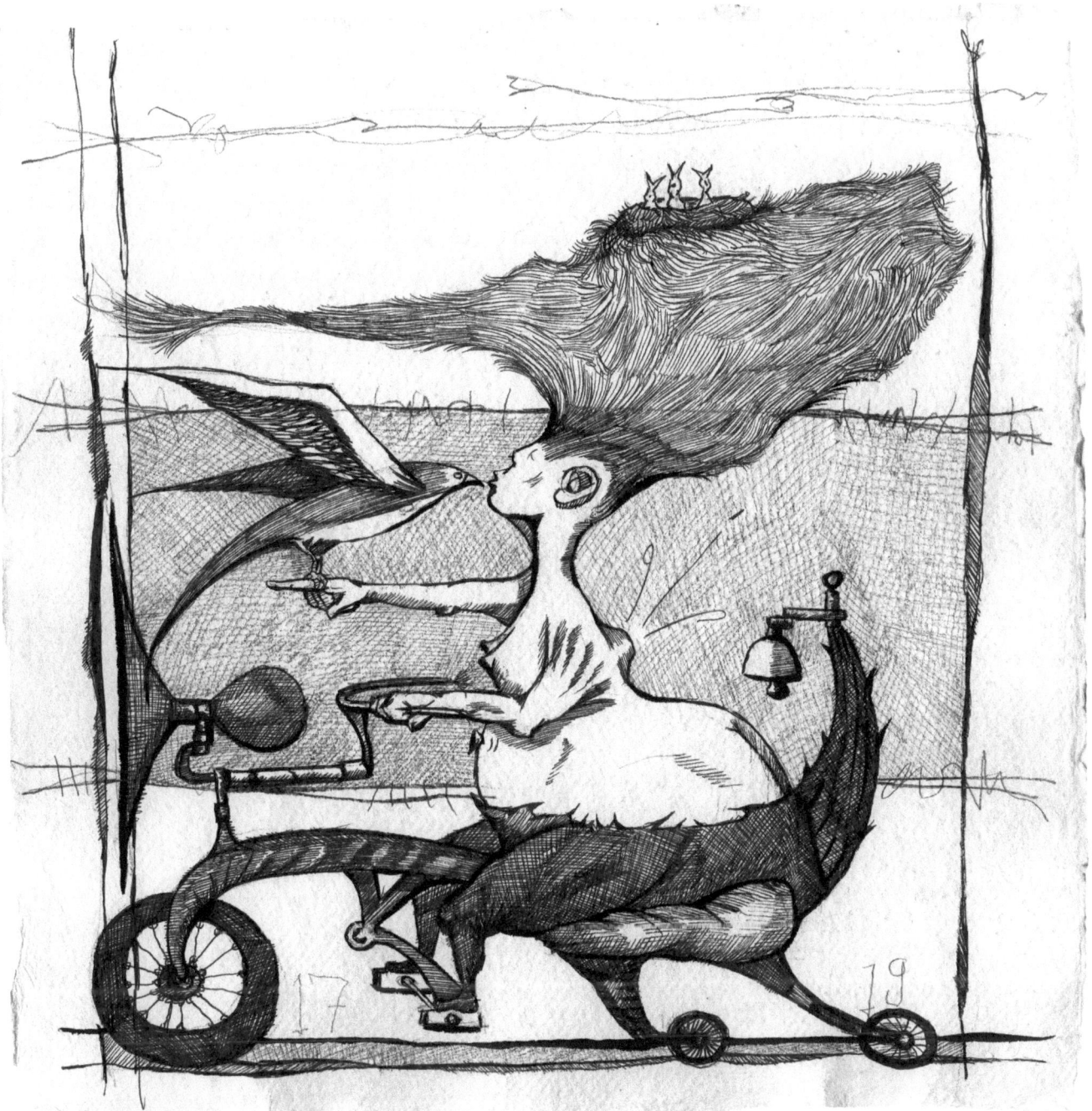

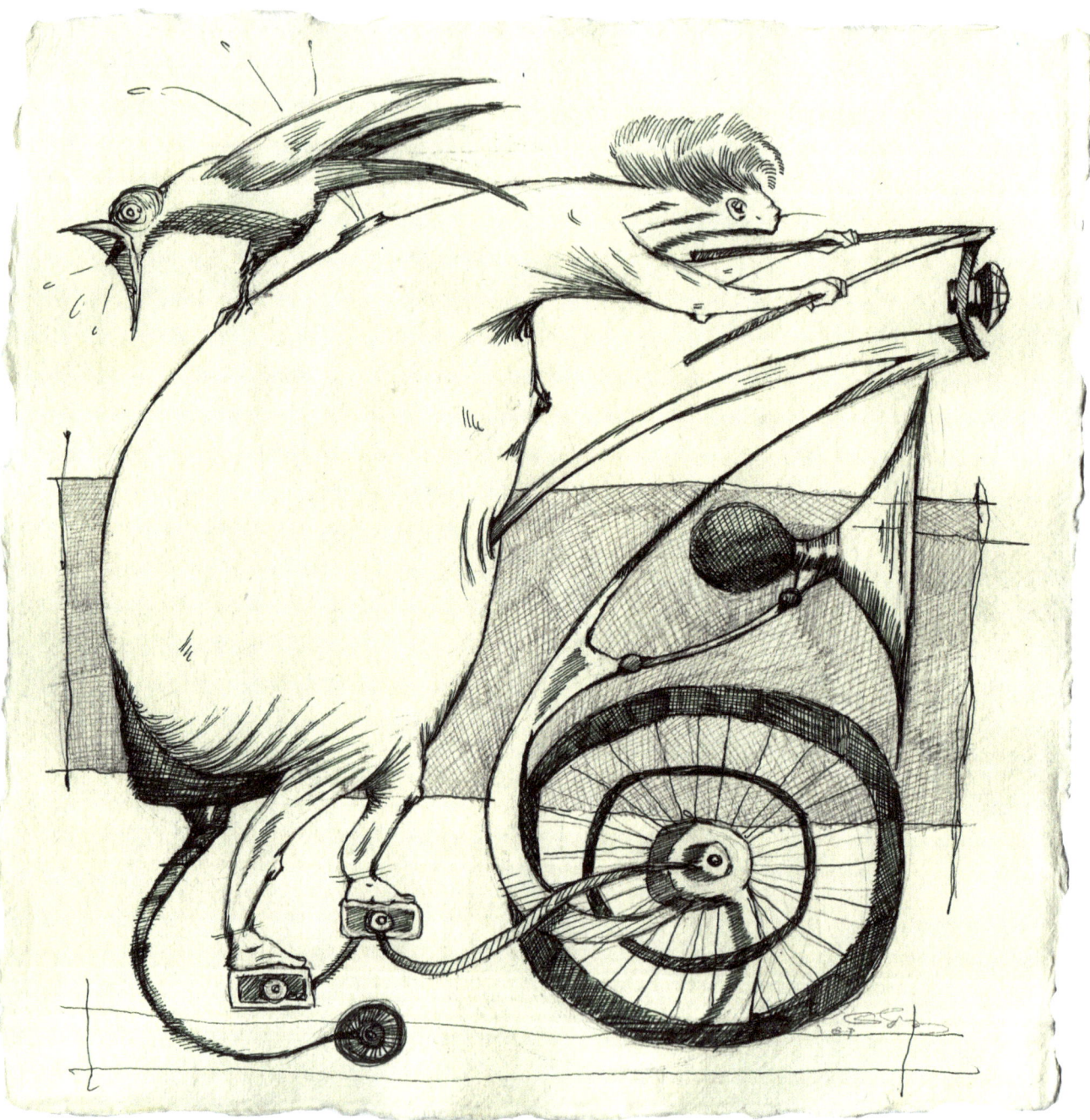

God loved the birds and made trees. Man loved the birds and invented cages.

Jacques Deval

My favorite memories are of the past, or this can't become a distant memory soon enough.

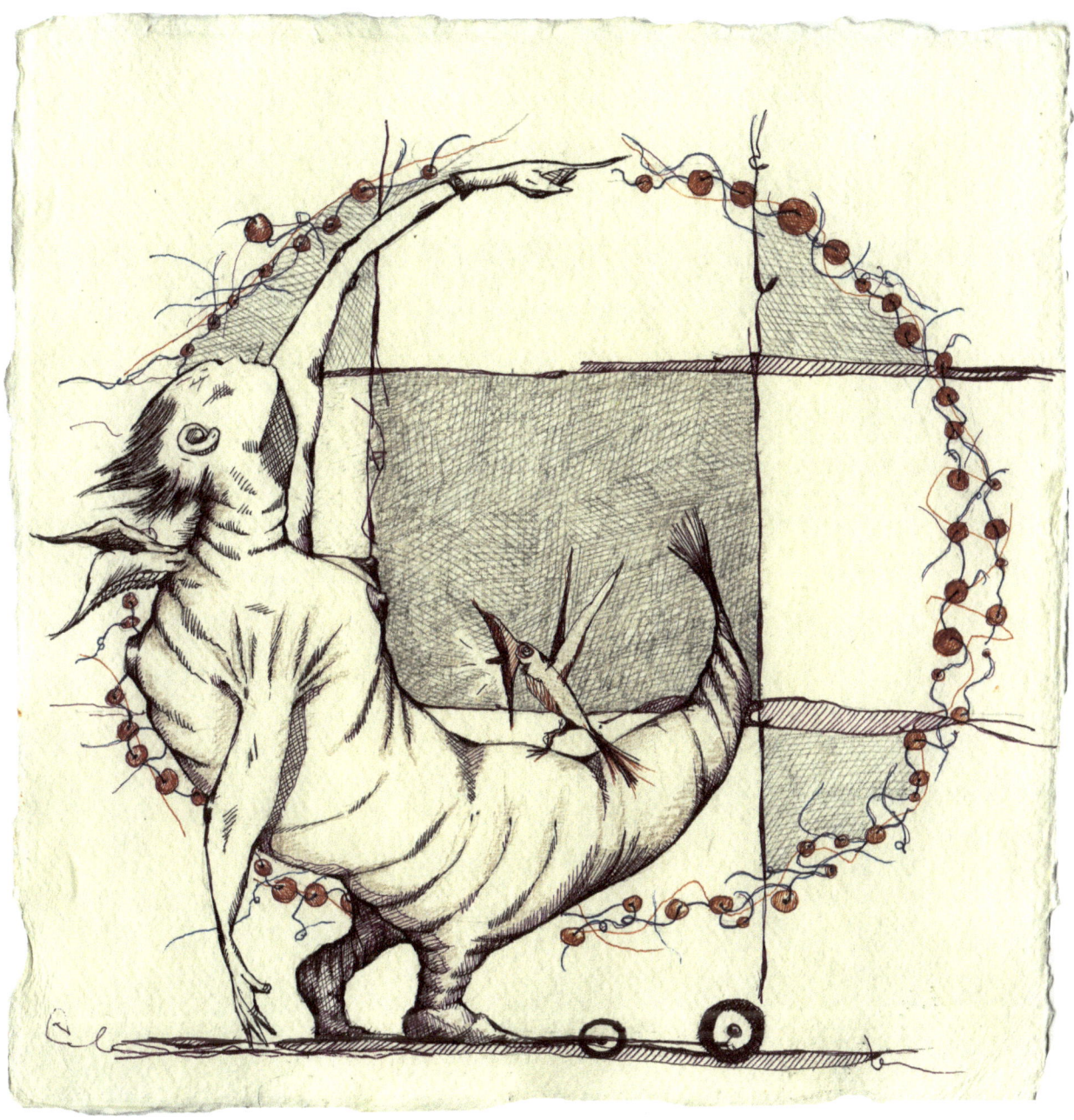

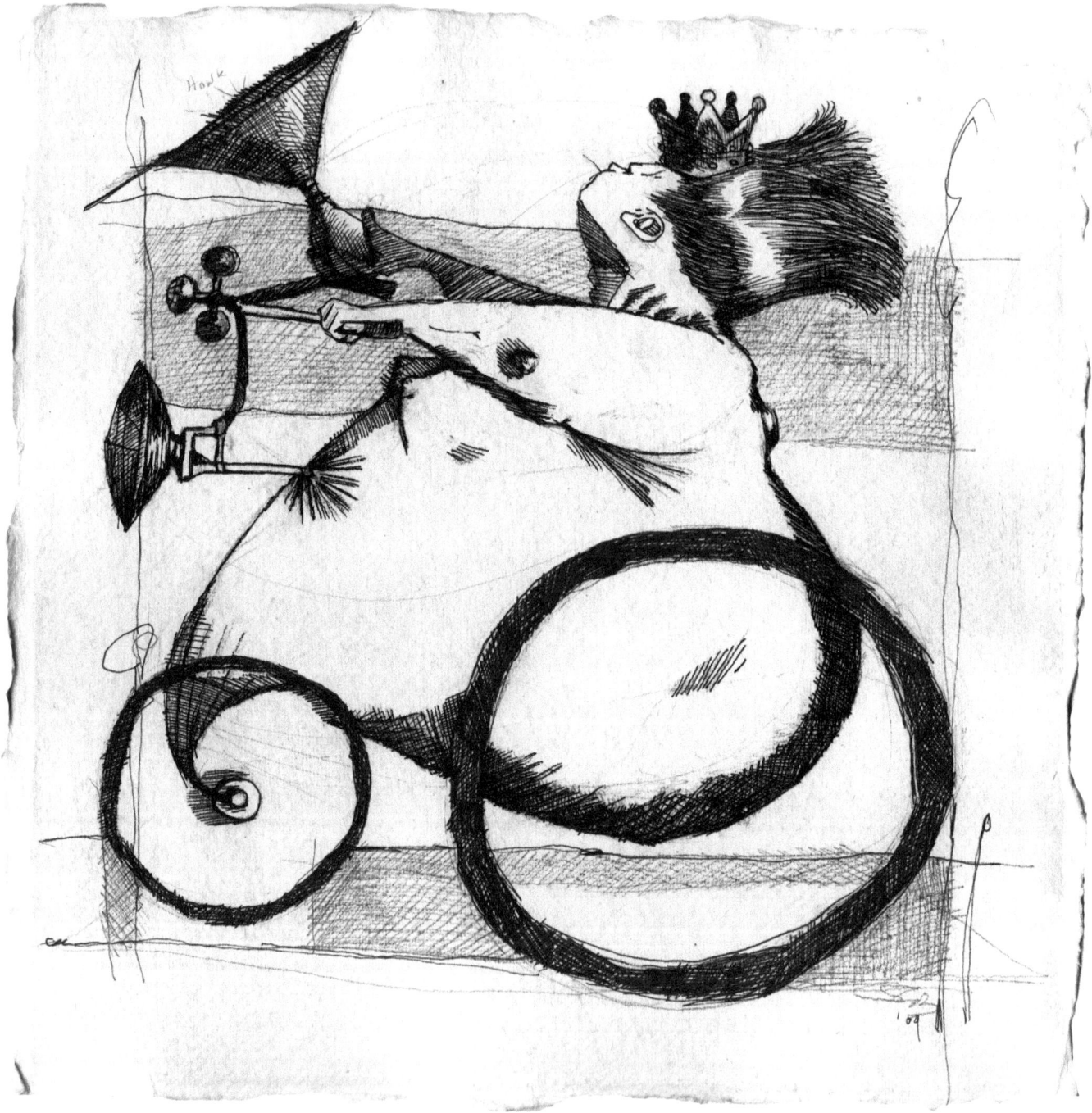

Don't let school interfere with your education.

I have kleptomania. When it gets bad I take something for it.

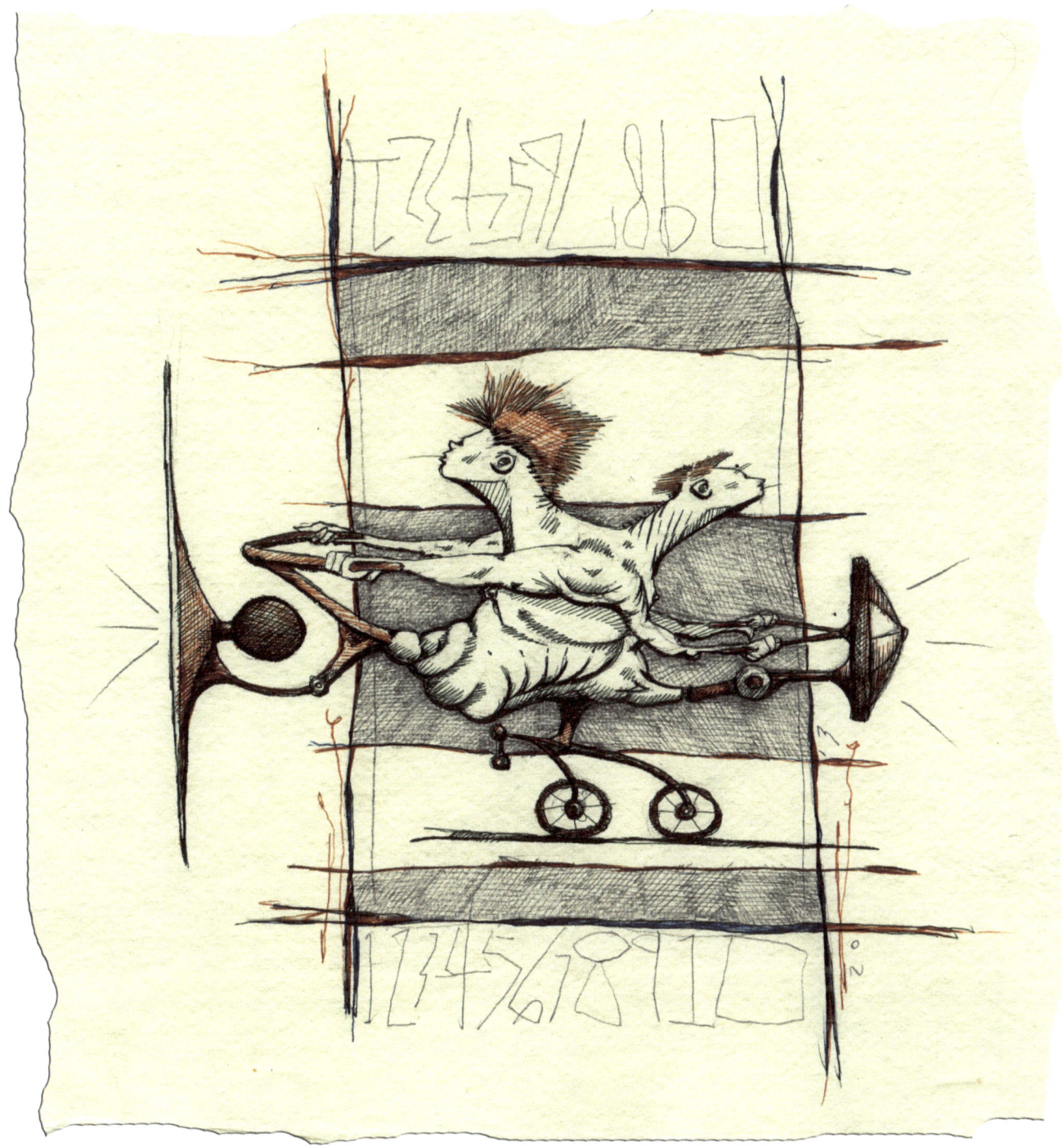

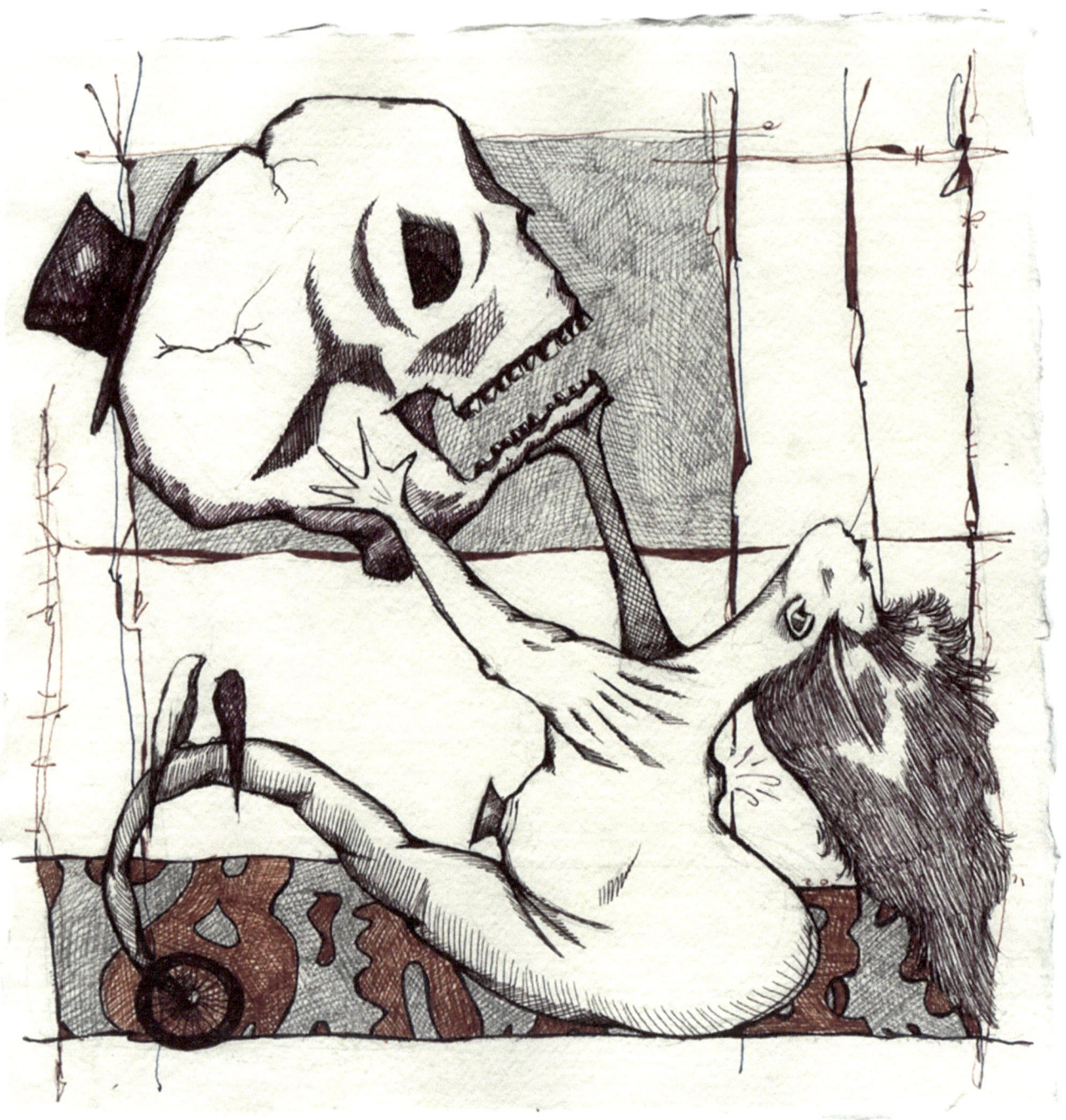

Kentucky: Five million people, fifteen last names.

Whatever hits the fan will not be evenly distributed.

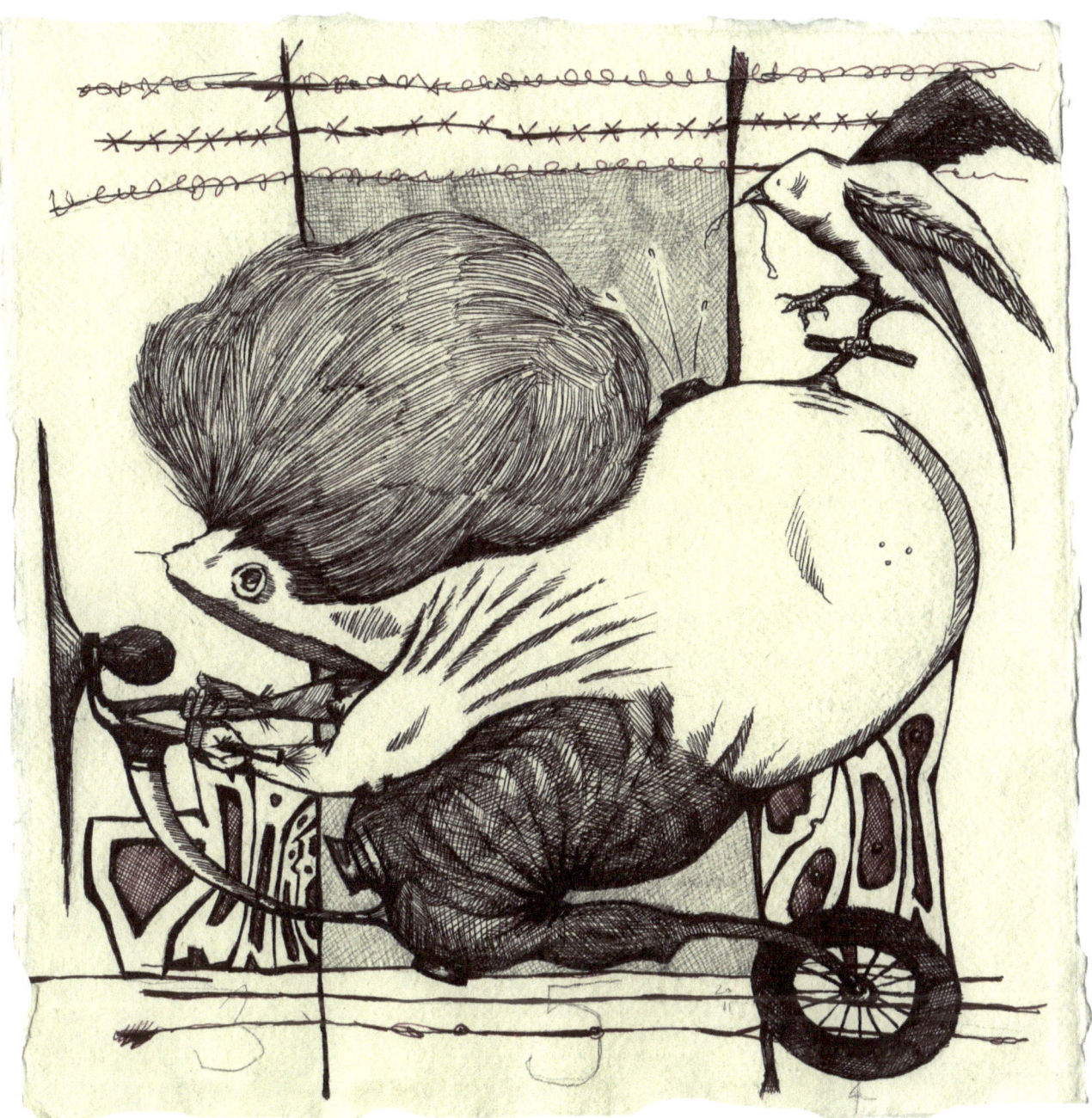

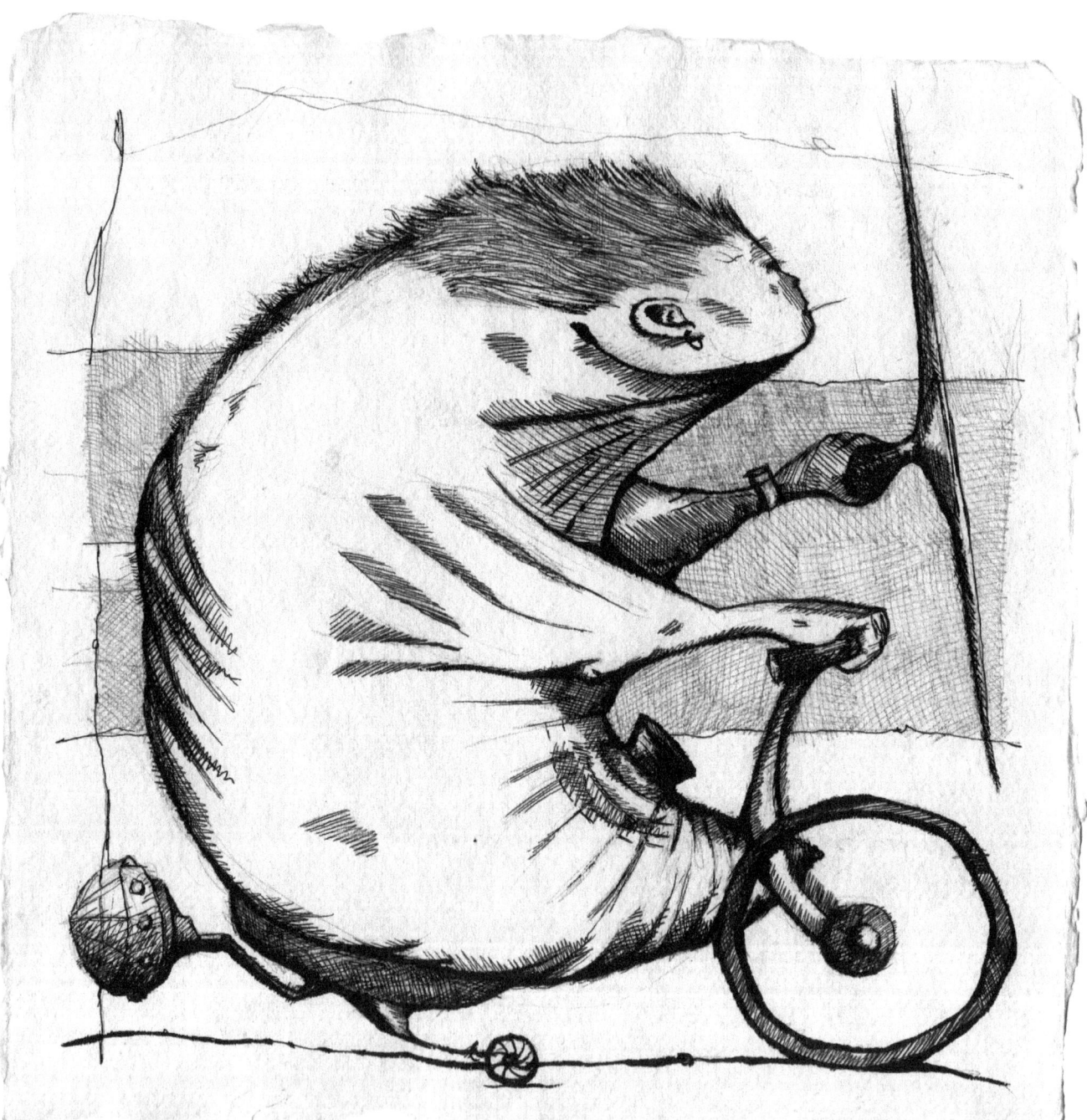

Just two days from now, tomorrow will be yesterday.

I used up all my sick days so I called in dead.

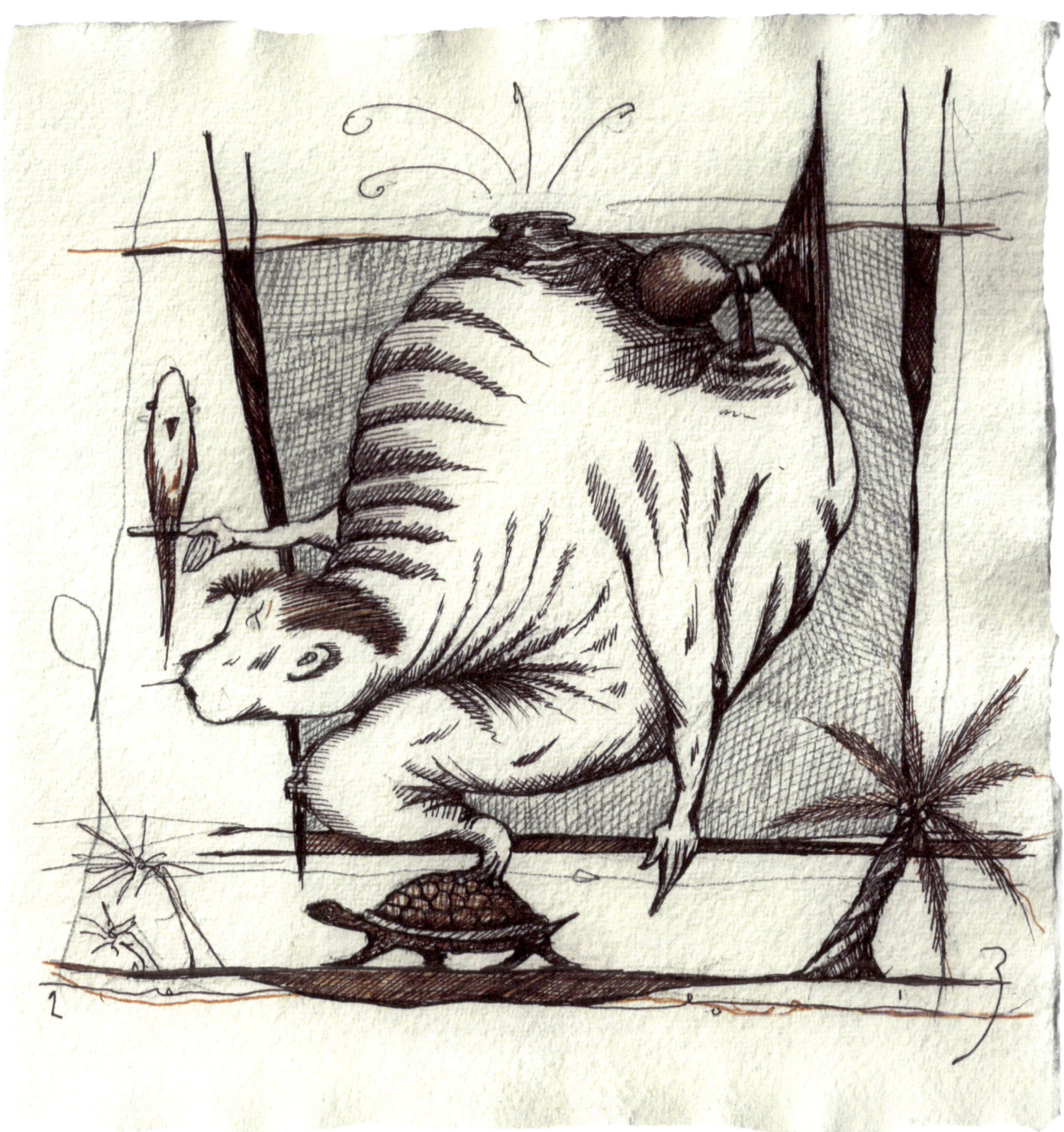

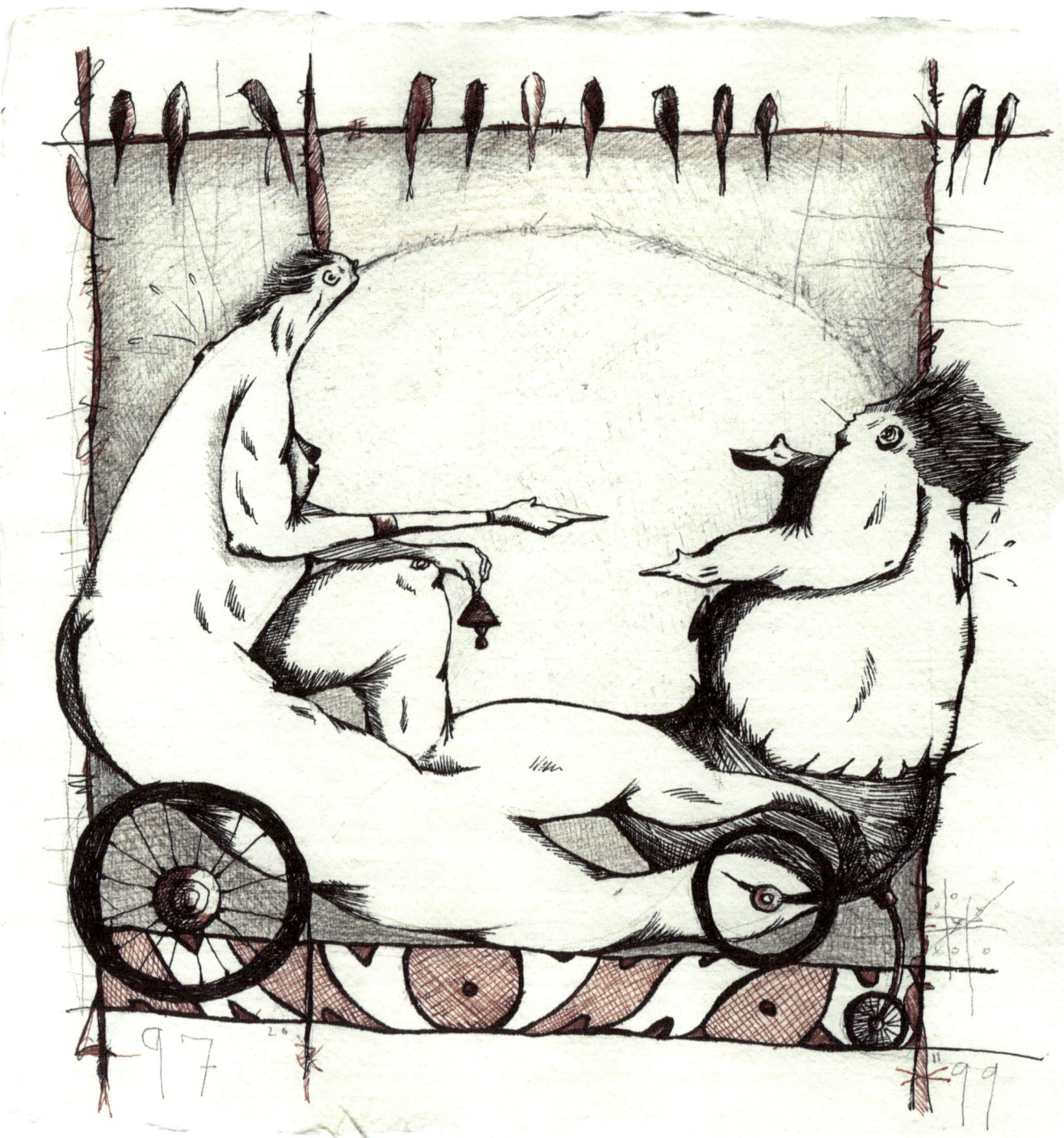

Suicidal twin kills sister by mistake.

Behind every successful man is a surprised woman.

Maryon Pearson

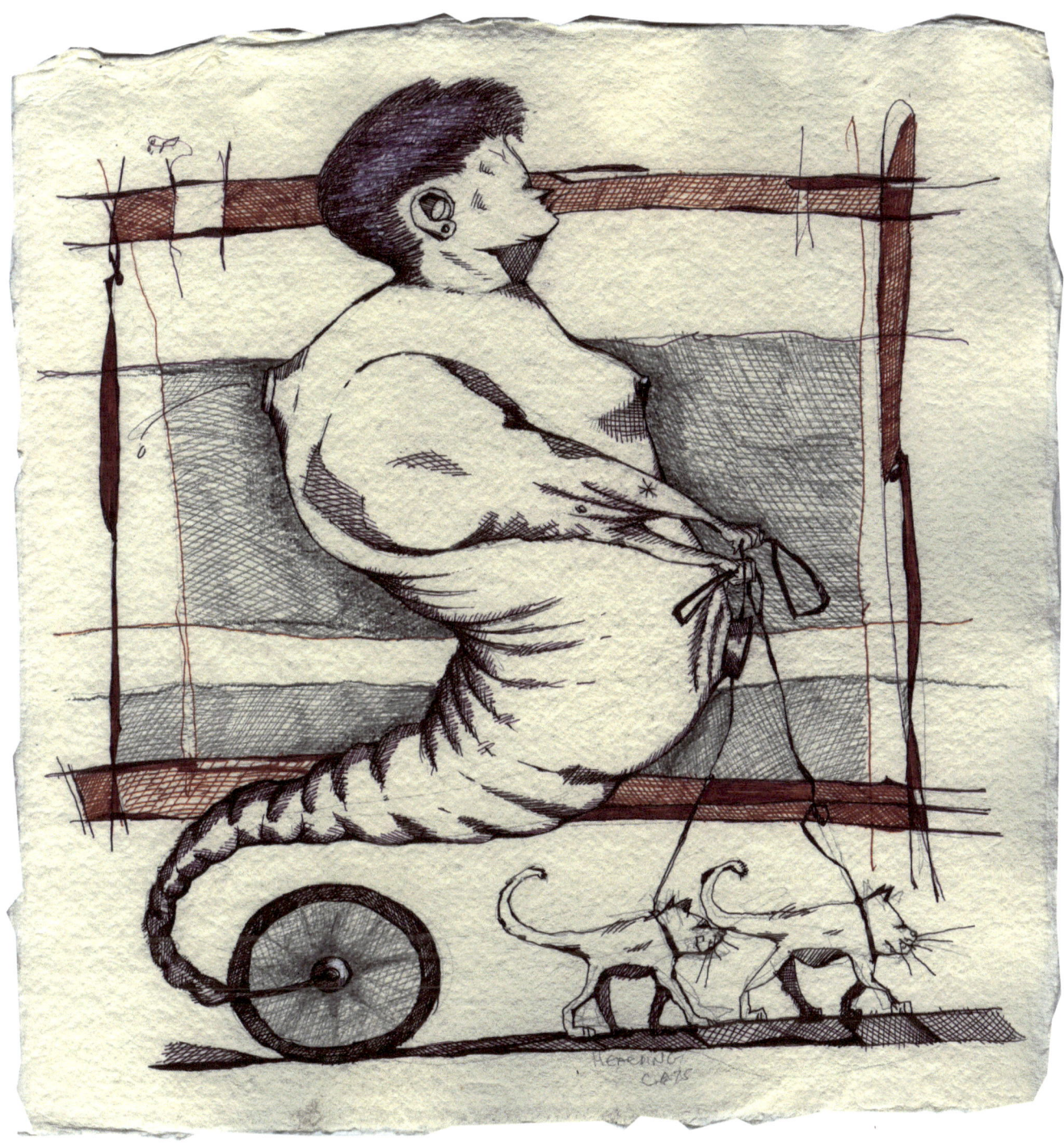

HERDING
CATS

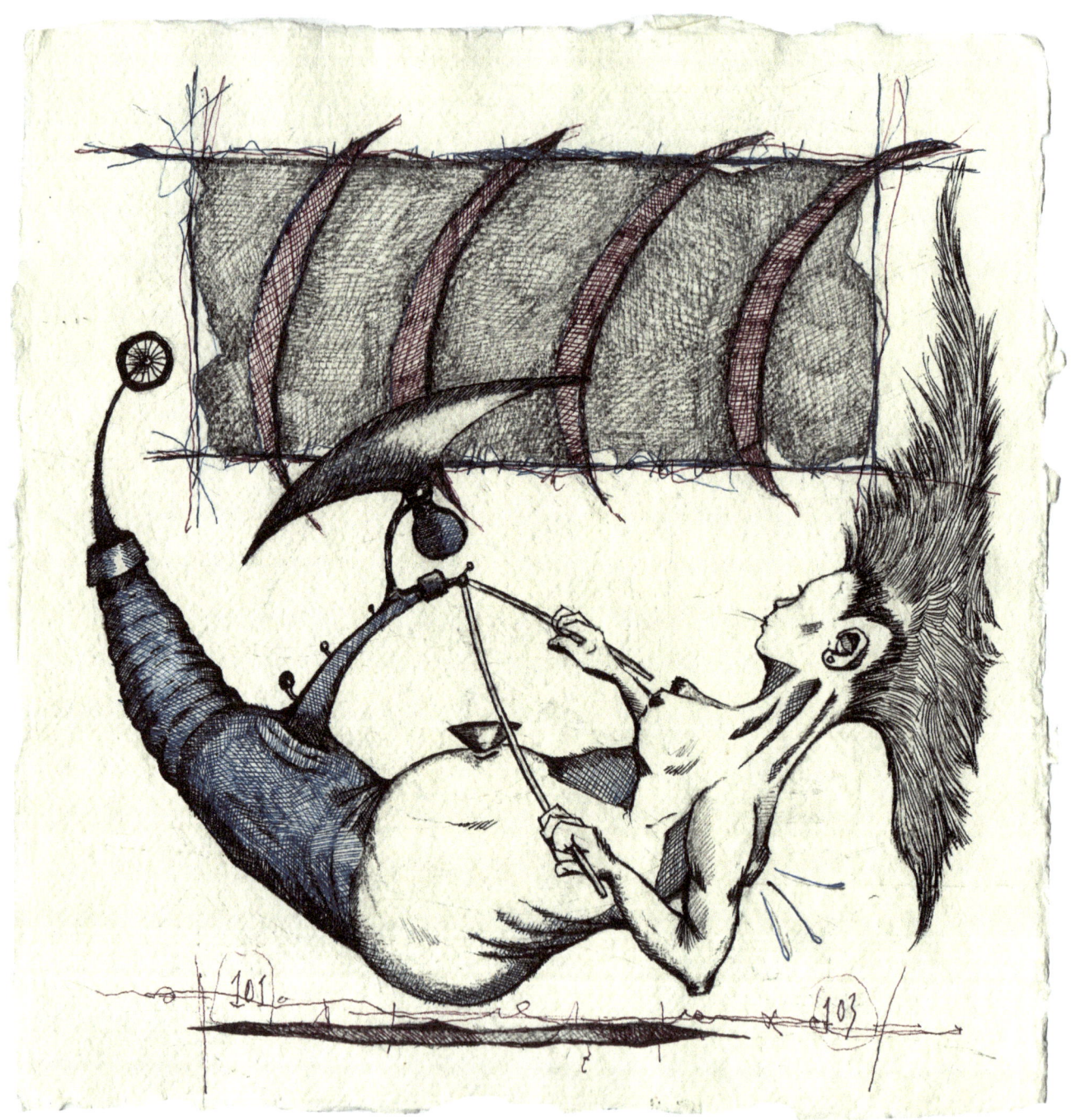

If you wait long enough science fiction will become reality.

If all else fails, stop using all else.

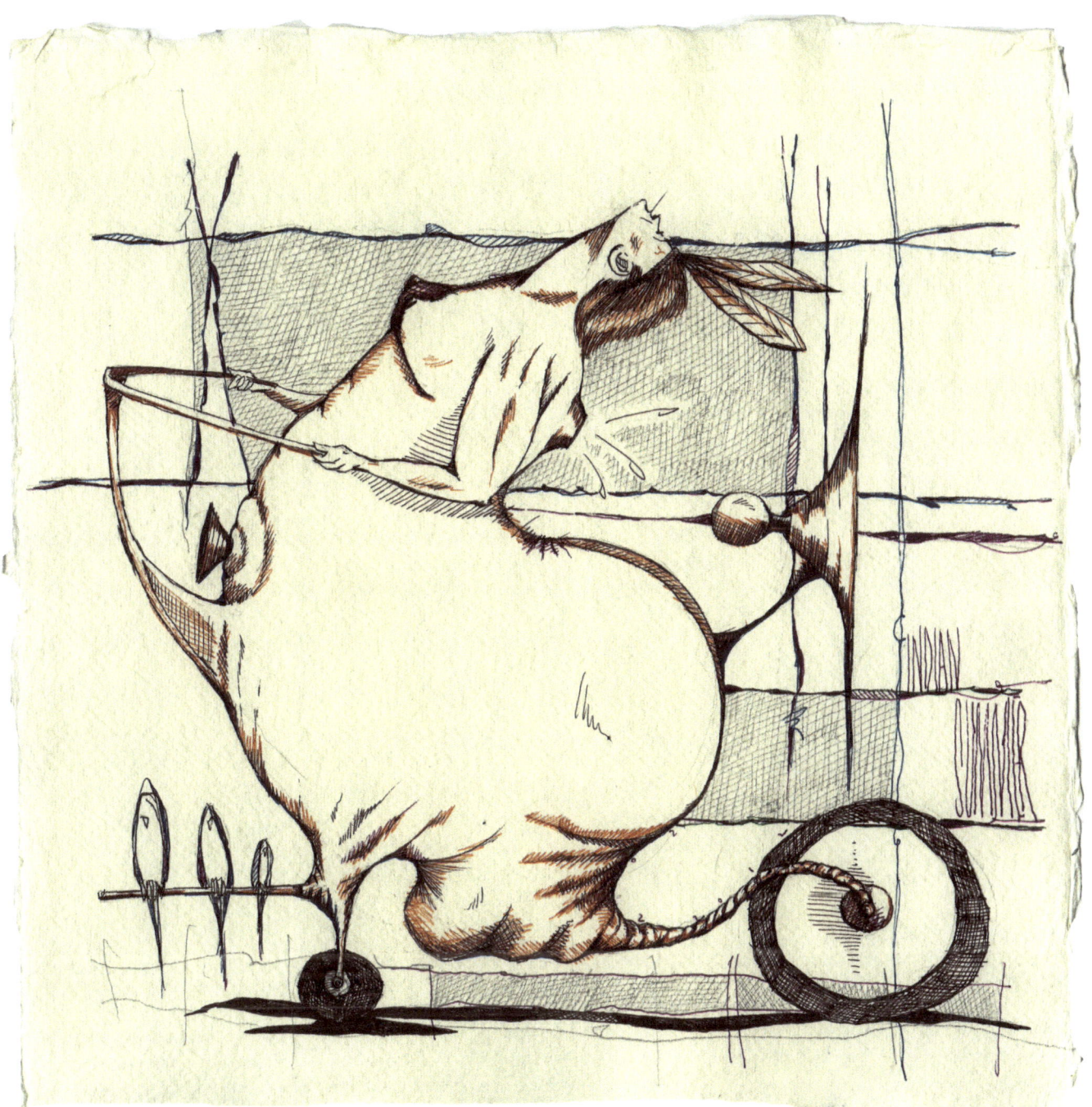

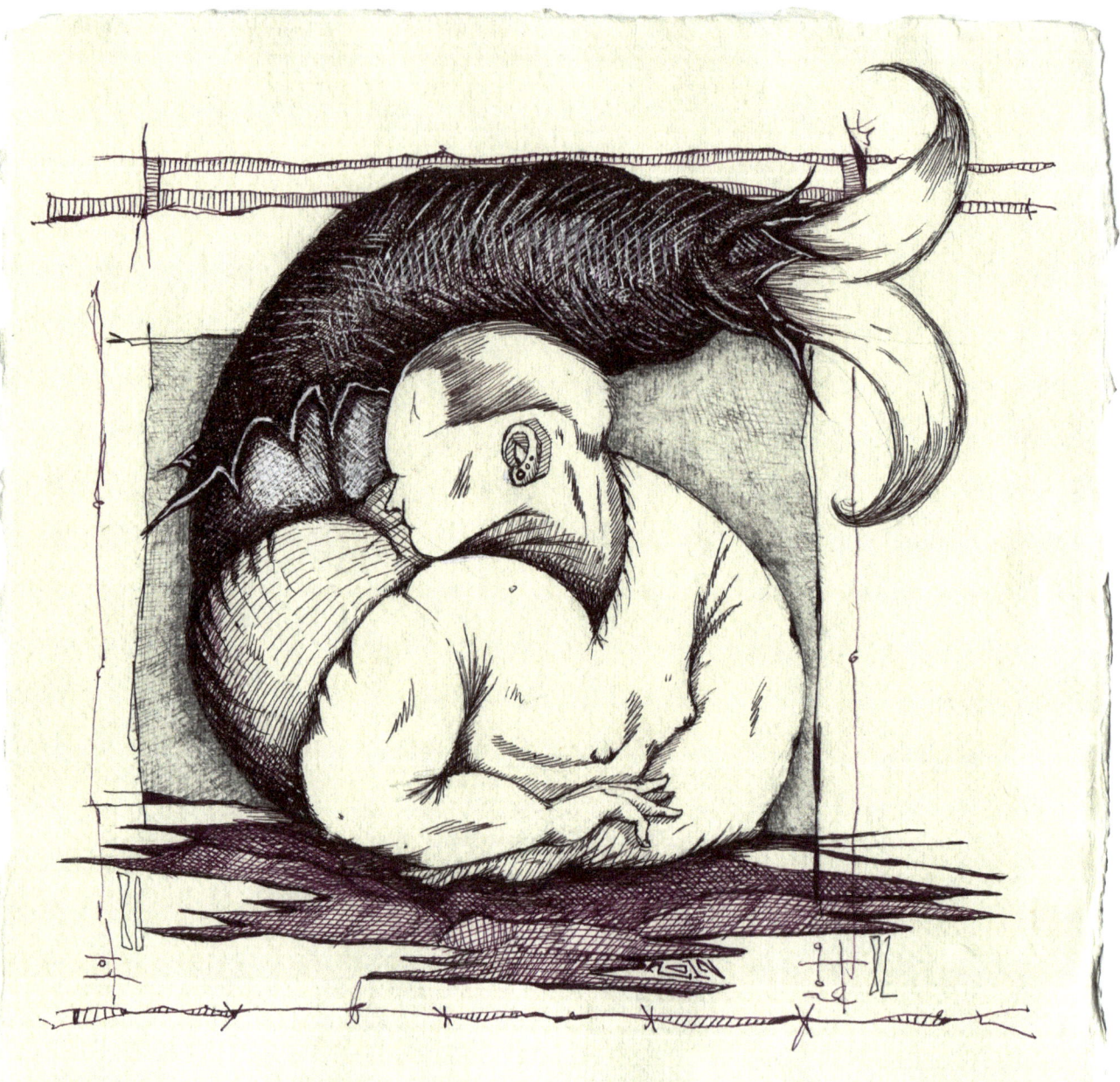

Don't sweat the petty things, don't pet the sweaty things.

George Carlin

Born and raised in Brooklyn, New York, Cheryl Gross is an illustrator, writer, motion-graphic artist, living and working in the New York/Jersey City area. She is a professor at Pratt Institute and Bloomfield College where she teaches her vocation.

Cheryl received her MFA from Pratt Institute. Her work has appeared in numerous films, TV shows, publications, and graces the walls of many corporate and museum collections including: The Body Electric, Fort Collins, Colorado, 2013,Filmpoem, Scotland, 2012, International Short Film Festival, Berlin, 2012, The Zebra International Poetry Film Festival, Berlin, 2012, 35th International San Francisco LGBT Film Festival, 100 New York Painters, Schiffler Publishing, Riverside Museum, Riverside, Ca., USA, The Museum of The City of New York, Mississippi Museum of Art, The New York Times, Comedynet.com, Associated Content.com, Current TV, Laforet Harajuku Museum, Tokyo, Japan, and Artist-In-Residency, Kunstlerhaus, Saarbruken, Germany.

Her illustration credits include; *Jimmy Stewart and His Poems*, Crown Publishing, *Circe*, Lowbrow Press, *Becoming Judas*, Red Hen Press, *In The Circus Of You*, Rose Metal Press, and *The Z Factor*, which she has written and illustrated.

When asked about her work:

"I equate my work with creating and building an environment, transforming my inner thoughts into reality. Beginning with the physical process, I work in layers. I am involved in solving visual and verbal complexities such as design and narrative. My urban influence has indeed added an 'edge' to my work."

Cheryl's work has often been compared to Dr. Seuss on crack.

VICTORY HALL PRESS
is a division of Victory Hall Inc.,
a not-for-profit arts organization
producing exhibitions, events,
education programs, public
projects and publications,
based in the NJ/NY metro area.

Other books include:

PORTRAIT PROJECT
Ross Bonn: 100 People

NEW DRAWING SERIES
presents series of innovative, current images
from artists whose work explores and expands
the visual and conceptual language of drawing.

Ibou Ndoye: Forms of Faces
Ibou Ndoye: Taarou Adaa
Jill Scipione: Skullnotebook
Carl Vierow: Detective at Red Castle Pier and Other Drawings
James Pustorino: Universechild
Hector G Romero: Last Coast Blues

To order copies: victoryhallpress.org

Victory Hall DRAWING ROOMS
180 Grand Street
Jersey City, N. J. 07302
www.victoryhall.org

To find out more about The Z Factor:
www.thezfactor.org
www.cmgross.com

www.ingramcontent.com/pod-product-compliance
Lightning Source LLC
Chambersburg PA
CBHW050741180526
45159CB00003B/1303